BV
3370
.17
V67
2017

Dear CRAIG,   Nov. 29 / '18

What a sincere honor to meet you & to fellowship together. Thank you for your spiritual leadership and your heart for the cities of our world.

IF I HAD

TWO LIVES

I trust that this story of my Dad will refresh & bless you!

THE EXTRAORDINARY LIFE AND FAITH OF COSTAS MACRIS

John Macris
jmacris@hellenicuntish.org

DAN VORM

Nyack College
Eastman Library

Clovercroft Publishing

D0291060

If I Had Two Lives: The Extraordinary Life and Faith of Costas Macris

©2017 by Dan Vorm

All rights reserved. No part of this book may be reproduced or transmitted in any form or by any means, electronic or mechanical, including photocopying, recording or by any information storage and retrieval system, without permission in writing from the copyright owner.

Published by Clovercroft Publishing, Franklin, Tennessee

Published in association with Larry Carpenter of Christian Book Services, LLC of Franklin, Tennessee

Unless otherwise designated, all Scripture quotations are from the *New American Standard Bible*, © Copyright The Lockman Foundation 1960,1962, 1963, 1968, 1971, 1972, 1973, 1975, 1977, 1988, 1995. Used by permission.

Scripture quotations marked (NLT) are from the *Holy Bible, New Living Translation*. Copyright © 1996. Used by permission of Tyndale House Publishers.

Scriptures marked (KJV) are from the *Holy Bible, Authorized Version*, public domain.

Cover Design by Kyle Macris

Author's photo by Larry Kayser

Interior Layout Design by Suzanne Lawing

ISBN: 978-1-942557-74-6

Printed in the United States of America

ENDORSEMENTS

My wife Nanci and I met Costas Macris in Greece in 1988, while I was a pastor visiting missionary friends from our church, Dan and Kerry Vorm. When Dan introduced me to Costas, I imagined I was prepared to meet this man whose visionary exploits in Indonesia I'd read about. After spending a few days around Costas I realized he was truly one of a kind. His energy, enthusiasm, and vision were contagious and compelling, at times entertaining, often breathtaking, and occasionally overwhelming. God raises up all kinds of people to accomplish His purposes, but on rare occasions you meet someone utterly unique, larger than life. Costas Macris was one of those. My old friend Dan Vorm skillfully tells the amazing story of this extraordinary servant of God.

—RANDY ALCORN, AUTHOR OF *HEAVEN, THE TREASURE PRINCIPLE,* AND *SAFELY HOME*

A truly amazing story of one of God's amazing men. I knew Costas, and he gave me the best opportunity I ever had to minister at a great mission's conference he organized. Reading this book, I feel I now know him and his wife so much better, and I give thanks to the LORD for their lives and this great ministry.

—GEORGE VERWER, FOUNDER AND FORMER INTERNATIONAL DIRECTOR OF OPERATION MOBILIZATION

If I Had Two Lives is the gripping saga of Costas and Alky Macris, a man and woman who served God not only faithfully but also ingeniously in one daunting arena after another. Joining World Team's missionary task force in West Papua, Costas and Alky contributed profoundly, first among Sawi cannibals in Papua's southern swamps, followed by another year confronting fearsome Yali warriors hidden away in some of Papua's loftiest mountain-walled valleys. Yet all of this was but a prelude to the ultimate challenge which Costas and Alky and their children had yet to face. A more inspiring testimony can hardly be found anywhere in the annals of Christian literature.

—DON RICHARDSON, AUTHOR OF *PEACE CHILD, LORDS OF THE EARTH, ETERNITY IN THEIR HEARTS,* AND OTHER TITLES.

Stories of courageous modern-day saints are hard to come by these days, but my friend Costas Macris fits the bill. I first met Costas in the 1980s when we ministered throughout Greece together. Warm and embracing, he saw every encounter as a divine appointment, as a chance to excitedly tell a new friend about Jesus. If you are looking for an older, wiser brother in Christ after whom you can model your faith, the remarkable story you hold in your hands will set the high bar. Filled with sage wisdom from a truly exceptional believer, *If I Had Two Lives* is your chance to sit at the feet of someone who knows what it means to die gladly to self and live victoriously to God.

—JONI EARECKSON TADA, JONI AND FRIENDS INTERNATIONAL DISABILITY CENTER

In a generation of trailblazing missionary titans, Costas Macris was himself a legend. I consider it one of the great privileges of my life to have known him and be inspired by him."

—STEVE RICHARDSON, PRESIDENT, PIONEERS USA

You will be thrilled as you read the amazing account of the Lord's work in and through Costas Macris among those Stone Age tribal people in what is now called Papua. I had the privilege to know the Macrises for many years and introduce Costas to missionary work...To God be the glory. Dig in and enjoy!

—DR. JOHN T. DEKKER – PARTNERS INTERNATIONAL

Reading *Two Lives* was like reading a 20th century continuation of the Acts of the Apostles. Surely, this could well be one of the most impacting books on missions of our time. This book, and Costas's life, humbles me, challenges me, and inspires me.

—DON STEPHENS, FOUNDER AND DIRECTOR, MERCY SHIPS

With the plethora of books now available it is rare to come across a book that stands out in the crowd. The story of Costas Macris is just such a book. It makes for a riveting read. The extraordinary life of Costas Macris demonstrates how with courage and determination and the blessing of the Lord remarkable things can be accomplished. You will want to get multiple copies of this book to pass along to others. It will impact many lives and is bound to become a missionary classic.

—NICO BOUGAS, HELLENIC MINISTRIES,
INTERNATIONAL DIRECTOR OF DEVELOPMENT;
EDITOR EMERITUS OF CHRISTIAN LIVING TODAY
MAGAZINE

CONTENTS

Part III: A Heart For His People

ACKNOWLEDGMENTS

In my opinion, the best Greek cooking involves many cooks in the kitchen. The sharing of spices and laughter—and the mingling of time-honored recipes—has a way of making the finished table that much tastier.

The same is true of this book.

Many people are due special thanks for their labor of love. Two special ladies deserve first mention. When a young Carlene Schlemeier first met Costas and Alky Macris in 1962, she was drawn to them and their work. She prayed for their ministry over the next forty-some years and took it upon herself to retain every newsletter, note, and personal letter. Carlene is now in heaven, but this book draws heavily from the overflowing files she left behind.

If Carlene was the record keeper, Kathryn Kline was the organizer. She and her husband, Paul, spent years colaboring with the Macris family in the jungles of Irian Jaya. They later joined the Macrises in Greece, where they continued as trusted and valuable coworkers. After Costas's death, Kathryn bore the vision—and weight—of this project. In her gracious yet determined way she e-mailed, researched, and willed this book to completion. If not for her detail-oriented diligence, it simply could not have been written. Thanks also to Paul and Kathryn for their careful editing and fact checking.

Special thanks, of course, to Alky Macris and the Macris children, whose faithful example and exuberant love for Christ have so deeply impacted me, my family, and untold others around the world. How I pray that this book will fittingly honor your beloved Costas.

Nico Bougas also deserves special recognition for pushing

this work forward, and for his encouragement and editorial skill. Thanks also to the many Macris friends and coworkers who shared experiences and anecdotes from throughout the years. Your colorful stories brought needed color and clarity. How Costas loved and esteemed each of you!

On the technical side, Larry Carpenter of Clovercroft Publishing has produced a beautiful volume. Special thanks to longtime friend and former colleague, Brian Smith, whose editorial skills greatly improved this manuscript. Thanks also to editor Tammy Kling of On Fire Publishing, to Suzanne Lawing for her great layout and to Gail Fallen for her copy-editing skills. As well, Denny Boultinghouse and Ramon Presson were kind to read initial drafts, sharing their time and expertise. Emily Doorandish used her inspirational creativity to provide beautiful maps and graphics. And Kyle Macris's excellent cover concept would surely have made his grandpa proud.

I also want to thank the many who consistently prayed for the completion of this book, including the men who meet with me weekly for Bible study, and the Fellowship Friday prayer group. The Lord has seen your significant contribution.

Of course, my wife, Kerry, and our four children deserve credit for their generous encouragement and patience. I'm such a blessed man. You all are the delight of my life.

The story of Costas's life is but one small thread in the glorious tapestry of God's redemptive plan. For this we give praise to our Lord Jesus Christ, who masterfully weaves our smaller stories into His majestic forever story. Only eternity will reveal the scope of its glory.

DEDICATION

To the many coworkers
in both Indonesia and Greece,
who shouldered the work at Costas's side.
No doubt he would consider this *your* story
as well as his.

And

To everyone who reads this story.
May God fan faith into flame,
and fill you with consuming vision
for the extraordinary things
He desires to do in and through you.

"If I had two lives to live, I would live one life for the people of Indonesia, and the other for the people of Greece."

COSTAS MACRIS
1935—2006

FOREWORD

by Eric Metaxas

I graduated Yale in 1984, wanting to be a writer, but for the next four years I was "at sea" over the direction of my life. I was lost. I didn't know my purpose or whether life had a purpose at all. I didn't know if there was a God or, if there was one, whether we could know Him. I certainly had no idea that we could know His will for our lives. Then in the summer of 1988 I had a dramatic born-again experience. It changed everything, and in newfound zeal for God I busied myself discovering and walking in His will.

In the summer of 1992 God supernaturally led me to Greece, for one of my many visits to my family in Cephalonia. I was zealous to tell everyone about what I had discovered. But I had grown up in the Greek Orthodox Church, and I knew that many Greeks would consider my new, exciting version of the Christian faith to be simply strange. They knew only of Greek Orthodoxy, and it struck me as a pity that so many had already dismissed Christianity as merely ritual. I was only there for a few weeks. Who would help them?

I wondered whether there were any evangelical churches I might visit. There had to be some born-again believers in Greece, but where were they hiding? Then I went to Athens, where I somehow connected with some born-again believers, and eventually with a man named Costas Macris. I was familiar with Don Richardson's book *Peace Child*, so when I learned that Costas was Richardson's partner in Irian Jaya and had shared in the experience described in the book, I was amazed. We went to his apartment and his office, and throughout that day he told me, with great energy, of some of his adventures over the years. When he learned that I was a writer, suddenly he focused on recruiting me to write his life story. One thing I learned that day: Costas Macris had a forceful personality. You don't live as a missionary among cannibals without qualities beyond the ordinary, and I saw that he did not give up easily. But eventually I convinced him that I had not yet written a full-length book, let alone a biography, and that I was not, at that time, up to the job. Clearly God had another plan for the book.

I came back to the United States and lived my life. Twenty-five years passed. I grew in the faith, got married, and had a daughter, and in time I finally began writing books. One day I was asked to write the foreword to this book. And I realized that, unbeknownst to anyone but me, it was the very book Costas had tried to persuade me to write twenty-five years ago! Who could fail to find that amazing and not a little humorous?

When I finally got down to reading this book, I saw that its author—the eminently capable Dan Vorm—knew far better than I had known, twenty-five years ago, how to tell the inspiring story of this man of God. I'm so glad Costas did not get his way in persuading me to do the job! This book tells in thrilling fashion how Costas Macris gave everything he had and risked his life many times to bring absolute strangers the good news of Jesus.

I know that some who read this tremendous book will be inspired to serve Jesus on the mission field. I also know that this book will inspire others to bring the good news of Jesus to Greece itself, a nation that has never before so badly needed the hope and peace that only the gospel can bring. (I pray that God will use me toward that end, too.) In fact, if you know someone of Greek background, why not give them a copy of this book? That might contribute to the Lord's work among Greeks.

Jesus was at work powerfully in the life of our brother, Costas Macris, as you will now see. And He is at work in our lives right now as we read this book. May it inspire you—and everyone to whom you give a copy—to glorious exploits for the kingdom of heaven. *O Theos mazi sou!*

ERIC METAXAS
January 2017
New York City

AUTHOR'S INTRODUCTION

The dry boredom of a ten-hour flight quickly subsided as our jet began its final approach toward Athens's Hellenikon International Airport. I looked out the airplane window, eyes wide with wonder. *So this is the Aegean Sea,* I thought as the plane cast its speeding shadow over sparkling waves. The morning sun was fresh upon the day, its brilliant light creating an aqua shimmer that stretched to meet the horizon.

The plane lumbered to a stop on the sun-drenched tarmac, and my twenty-one-year-old mind raced with excitement. *Could it be I am really in Athens, Greece?*

The trip had been conceived months before in the student dining hall at Chicago's Moody Bible Institute. At dinner one evening I met an impressive first-year student named Johnathan, with a fascinating story. He had been raised in the jungles of Irian Jaya, Indonesia, where his family had lived among Stone Age tribes for sixteen years. They then returned to their native Greece, where his parents established a missionary organization.

I was captivated by Johnathan's stories, especially when I saw pictures of the ministry in Athens. Before the night was over, Johnathan had thrown down a challenge: "Dan, you sing and play guitar. Why don't we gather some students, form a music team, then spend next summer ministering in Greece?"

For a boy from suburban Oregon, this was heady stuff. Yet God was in it, and by the following July our small music team, the Disciples, was flying from New York to Athens. My Greece adventure had begun.

Many impressions from that summer of 1982 remain

etched in my mind—the stark beauty of the land and sea, the warmth and hospitality of the Greek people, the pungent smells of Greek cooking, and the boldness of the Greek evangelical believers.

And the history. Oh, what history! From Socrates to Euripides, from Alexander the Great to the footsteps of Paul in first-century cities. It seemed each dusty step I took was a journey into a panoramic, living encyclopedia.

Yet the summer's greatest impact came from watching Johnathan's family in action, and especially his father, Costas. I'd never encountered such a man.

Costas Macris was a rare combination of charisma and lack of self-importance, truly a man without guile. Yet with his flashing eyes and unhindered laughter, combined with God-given force of personality, he filled every room that he entered.

Here was a man on a mission! Always dreaming. Rarely pausing. Constantly pushing. A blur of activity and vision, compassionate at his core. He possessed childlike faith, daring to believe God would act, then rejoicing with full-throated delight when He did.

I wondered in what ways I could be like him. He was larger than life, I had a quiet demeanor. He was a dynamic leader, I felt part of the crowd. He was often loud and domineering and sometimes made me uncomfortable. Yet I was drawn to his faith and the way God honored his outlandish trust. At summer's end I returned to school, Costas's unique example fresh in my mind.

Several years later I again arrived in Athens to join Costas's ministry, this time with my precious wife at my side and youthful zeal in my chest. As full-time workers we immersed ourselves in the Greek language and culture, and were lovingly adopted by the Macris family's organization, Hellenic Missionary Union (HMU, later changed to Hellenic Ministries).

For the next season of our lives we worked closely with

Costas. We grew to dearly love and respect him. We observed his great tenderness and compassion. We were also confronted with his weaknesses. Strong of will, eyes always forward, he sometimes bulldozed those in his way. He could be stubborn and unswerving. Yet the hand of God was upon him, and when tempted to criticize, I felt rather like Michal, wife of King David. In confronting her husband's dancing unclothed in the streets, her scorn had merit, yet it fell on a man whose exuberance revealed a life anointed by God.

After five years in Greece we returned to the States to pursue pastoral ministry. Yet the lessons I learned at Costas's side have never left me. Among them:

Trust God for great things, and celebrate when He comes through.

Be the first to jump in, and lead by example.

Work harder than you think possible.

Embrace people with God's love, even when it's messy.

The example of Costas's extraordinary life and faith has been a great encouragement for my walk with Christ. I pray the same for you, dear friend, as you read the story of this unique servant of God.

DAN VORM
Nashville, Tennessee

PROLOGUE

The warrior stood proudly high on the mountainside, guarding the entrance to his village. Eyes narrowed to slits, he scanned the trail below. He creased his face in a defiant scowl. His muscles tensed, readying for a fight. His dark skin glistened in the morning sun. He wore a cowrie-shell necklace, and a small boar's tusk protruded from his flaring nostrils. A multicolored plumage of feathers towered high above his brow, tufts of dried grass and feathers hanging down each side of his head to his shoulders. He gripped a bow in one hand, an arrow in the other.

"Get ready!" he shouted to his fighting companions. "I see them coming." They grunted acknowledgment, then dug their toes into the soft dirt, forming a line to block the way.

The warrior watched a small group of men making their way, single file, up the narrow mountain trail. As expected, the white-skinned intruder—man or ghost, he wasn't sure—was leading the way.

The warrior—a respected witch doctor—swore an oath under his breath. How dare this unwelcome visitor invade their village and threaten their long-held traditions? The warrior had seen the danger firsthand—his own son had been influenced by this stranger's teachings.

The group approached. The warrior leaped onto a stone wall and raised his weapon. He steadied his bow, then threaded the arrow and drew it back tight. He took aim at the white-skinned enemy.

*   *   *

Alky Macris gasped in fear. From a small house built next to a primitive airstrip, she watched the unfolding drama across a small valley. Through unsteady binoculars she followed the men's final ascent toward the mountain village. Now suddenly she heard shouting and saw commotion, but she was too far away to see details.

She had no idea that her missionary husband, Costas, had a warrior's arrow pointed directly at his chest.

PART I
BEGINNINGS

CHAPTER 1

A TALE TO TELL

September 25, 1963, dawned with a crisp fall morning at Flushing Meadows, New York. A small group of dignitaries took turns behind a makeshift podium on a portable stage, adorned with Greek and American flags, one on each side. The Greek delegation thrust shovels into the ground and turned over soil that would soon give way to the gleaming Pavilion of Greece, a monument to the glories of the Hellenic State, past and present. The 1964 New York World's Fair was quickly rising from the marshy meadows, one exotic structure at a time. Greece was excited to take part. This small, proud nation joined fifty-seven others, as well as many large international corporations, in building extravagant pavilions for showcasing mankind's greatest achievements.

When the fair's director of international exhibits took his turn behind the podium, he singled out one Greek official for special mention: "One man in particular has been the power behind the scenes. He's my longtime friend, Mr. Macris. He is the head of European Displays, Limited, in Athens. . . . We contacted him and he went to bat for us; we certainly can say that he has batted a thousand. He is now managing director of the Greek Pavilion and is its prime architect."

Athanase Macris, known to friends and family as Thanos, smiled and nodded at the polite applause. He was grateful for the recognition but anxious for construction to begin. The project had required two years already, and he was excited to see his architectural drawings spring to life.

Over the next two years the pavilion proved a success. By the fair's end in October 1965, millions of visitors had toured the pavilion and experienced the rich culture, history, industry, and flavors of Greece. Thanos Macris returned home to Athens an architectural success. He would go on to design many more exhibits and even museums in Greece and abroad.

ATHENIAN ROOTS

L to R: Young Costas, sister Marina,
parents Thanos and Jeni, brother Nikos.

Thanos's father hailed from the large port city of Patras, a sprawling community on the country's southwestern flank, considered Greece's gateway to the West. His mother's side were refugees from Asia Minor. Thanos was raised in Athens, where he met and married his wife, Jeni, and raised their four children.

Their eldest was a daughter, Manon, born when Thanos was just nineteen. Next came Nikos, followed by Marina. Two years after Marina, in June 1935, the fourth Macris child entered the world.

They named him Costas.

The young child seemed healthy at first, but within months he contracted a life-threatening disease, for which there was no known cure. Penicillin had not arrived in Greece, and vaccinations and other antibiotics were yet in the future. The doctor gave slim hope that young Costas would survive, so the devastated family prepared for the worst. Jeni gathered cloths with which to wrap the infant's body once he died.

Thanos, at a point of despair, took the child in his arms and prayed aloud. To that point in his life he had given little attention to spiritual things. In fact, he wasn't at all sure that God existed. Still, he held little Costas outstretched and said, "God, if You exist, and if You spare the child's life, I will give him to You."

In desperation, the doctor tried something unusual. He injected a petroleum substance into the infant's leg. Whether this was a known remedy or just an innovative physician's hunch, we don't know. Unexpectedly, and to the family's great relief, the child began to heal. Within weeks Costas was out of danger.

This was not the only threat Costas would face during his childhood years. At the time of his birth the winds of war were rising throughout Europe. In 1941, as Costas turned six, the Nazi storm had overrun the major cities of Greece. The swastika's placement over the ancient Acropolis was an ominous sign for the people of Athens. Indeed the Greeks would suffer three years under the jackboots of the brutal Nazi regime.

The German occupation dragged on, and life became increasingly difficult. Food became scarce, and many of Athens's 2.5 million inhabitants faced the threat of starvation. Fortunately, the Macris family always had food on the table, if not much, while many around them suffered. Thanos often shared food with friends and neighbors, even strangers. This example of generosity would influence Costas for the rest of his days.

The stench of death was all around. Costas and his siblings remembered sitting on their balcony, watching trucks loaded with dead bodies rumble through the streets below. Bodies were sometimes seen in the streets, casualties of war and famine. In spite of the inescapable trauma, Costas remembered a happy childhood. When spare change remained after buying necessities, his father, driven by an inexhaustible love of learning, often patronized the local bookstore, buying volumes to add to his large home library.

The children enjoyed a dinnertime ritual: They would sit at the table asking their father questions—about anything that came to mind—and he would do his best to answer. This instilled in the family creativity and a love of knowledge that would serve them throughout their lives.

Costas, the youngest, was loved by his protective siblings. They considered him the cutest and took pride in him as he grew. An average student, he worked hard and developed good character. He had his naughty moments, like any child, but was mostly obedient and respectful to authority.

By the time Germany and Bulgaria were forced to withdraw from Greece in early October 1944, much of the country lay in ruins. Tens of thousands had succumbed to starvation, most of the country's infrastructure had been destroyed, and most industries were incapacitated. Within months political polarization led to civil war, which lasted until the end of 1949. Thus by age fourteen Costas had lived nearly a decade in the context of war.

Perhaps the most remarkable feature of Costas's early years is that they left him largely unmarked, considering the atrocities occurring just outside his door. A warm family full of love, creativity, and intellectual curiosity provided a nurturing space for him to develop. He also exemplifies the human capacity to survive—even thrive—though surrounded by uncertainty and chaos. As is true of many, tragic events served to strengthen Costas's character rather than leave him defeated.

A PERSONAL CONVERSION

Sometime before the war Thanos Macris befriended a business associate who attended an evangelical church. Though evangelicals were considered heretics by most in the Orthodox Church, Thanos felt drawn to the personal nature of his friend's walk with God. After many soul-searching conversations that led to a fresh interest in reading the Bible, this once-proud agnostic began to understand Christianity in a new way. Religion had seemed distant and impersonal to his inquiring mind; he now learned that a relationship with God could be vital and dynamic. Before long, the family was attending Athens's First Evangelical Church, and Thanos received Jesus Christ as his Lord and Savior.

Consequently, Costas and his siblings attended evangelical youth camps during their teens. These summer camps were fun, especially after the travesty of war. And they provided something even more valuable—the gospel. Costas had seen a change in his father's life, and this sparked a curiosity about spiritual things. At camp, away from the distractions of city life and normal routines, Costas listened intently to the daily Bible teaching.

During his fourteenth year, a camp experience changed Costas's life forever. Having contracted tuberculosis, he was assigned to help the camp nurse ration out feta cheese that had been donated by the United States government. When the nurse, Mrs. Karboni, challenged him to believe that Christ died and rose again to be his personal Savior, Costas took it to heart. Later that evening, in the quietness of his tent, he surrendered his life to God. Instantly he knew his sins had been forgiven. He also knew he would live with Jesus forever in heaven.

Over the following weeks and months his experience confirmed the Bible's teaching. God's Word became alive to him as never before, and he sensed his life changing from the inside out. This was not a temporary spiritual high—he had made a decision that would determine the course of his life. In his youthful zeal he even decided to part his hair on the opposite side, determined that everything would be different!

Another of life's biggest decisions was not far in the future, regarding a pretty young girl named Alky.

CHAPTER 2

HALCYON DAYS
OF LOVE

The young girl in her bright summer dress caught Costas's eye.

He attended Athens's First Greek Evangelical Church. She attended Second Greek Evangelical Church. But both communities were small and mixed regularly. This made Costas glad—he could spend more time getting to know this sweet girl, Alky.

He learned her grandparents were Greeks from Asia Minor and had fled for their lives during the Asia Minor Catastrophe, when ethnic cleansing by the Turks caused a massive refugee migration in the early 1920s. While in Asia Minor, Alky's grandfather had been responsible for supplying food to an American-sponsored orphanage. After the Catastrophe, when the orphanage relocated to the Greek island of Syros, both of Alky's grandparents moved to Greece as refugees. Several years later Alky's father and mother met while working in the orphanage office. Before long the couple was married and living in Athens. There they raised their precious Alky in the warm embrace of Athens's evangelical community.

Costas and his older brother, Nikos, were handsome young teenagers, and they dressed with flair. The church girls couldn't help but take notice. But it was Costas's spiritual zeal that impressed Alky most. When he talked about going into ministry, she couldn't help dreaming about her future. The wife of a well-known pastor shared Alky's name, and she found herself thinking, *Perhaps I will be a pastor's wife, like her.*

By the time Costas and Alky finished high school, they were dating seriously. They had to meet secretly, however, for Alky's parents didn't favor the relationship. For this reason they sent her to Cyprus to live with relatives and study at an American academy, not realizing that Costas had just left for Bible college in Canada. The young couple corresponded, and their relationship flourished through their letters.

A CALLING MADE CLEAR

Costas's original plan had been to study in England, following in the steps of his pastor. But a traveling evangelist influenced him instead to choose Millar Memorial Bible Institute in Saskatchewan. So in fall 1954, at eighteen, Costas found himself surrounded by windswept wheat fields on the plains of southern Canada.

For a city boy from Athens, life in rural Canada took getting used to. One morning a mouse scampered across his classroom floor. Costas jumped onto his chair, while a sturdy farm girl cornered the rodent, grabbed it by its tail, and threw it out the window. He knew he was far from home. And though

Costas in Saskatchewan at Millar Bible Institute

Athens can get chilly in winter, Saskatchewan offered cold on a whole new level. Costas sometimes wondered if Canada had enough blankets to keep him warm.

But the freezing winters did little to chill the warming of his heart toward missions. Millar, with its faithful Bible teaching and invigorating student life, was a greenhouse for growing missionary zeal. When an unusually powerful chapel speaker challenged the students to go to the ends of the earth with the gospel, Costas felt a stirring in his chest. *Lord,* he prayed, *is this Your call for my life? Could You use me to take the gospel to those who've never heard?*

The speaker encouraged the students to kneel before the Lord in their room and not get up until willing to follow Christ in whole-hearted obedience. That night Costas knelt by his bed, laying his open Bible before him. Hour after hour he cried out to God. "Lord, what is Your will for my life? I feel a stirring in my heart toward missions. Is this Your call for me?"

All through the night Costas knocked at heaven's door, determined to hear God's answer. "I will not get off my knees, Lord, until I know for sure. I must know Your call upon my life!"

Sometime in the early morning Costas believed he had his reply. A deep assurance washed over him, an inexplicable peace and joy, a decisive clarity, on which he would lean for the rest of his days. Through tears he opened his hands and his heart in reverent submission. He knew what he was created to do. "Yes, Lord," he prayed softly, "I will take the gospel to the ends of the earth."

Alky, now back in Athens after her year in Cyprus, wasn't surprised by Costas's newfound clarity. He had previously written from Canada, informing both her and his family that he desired to be a missionary. But Costas's perception of God's clear call made the dream suddenly more real, prompting the obvious next question: Was God calling her to the same life?

Costas returned in 1957. Their love for each other had grown exponentially, and they talked seriously of marriage. The issue of calling loomed large before them. They decided Alky should attend Millar on her own, where she might determine God's direction for her life.

Alky's parents were less than excited. It was hard to see their daughter leave for Canada, but the idea of her marrying a missionary was even more difficult to take. Costas wanted to come to their house to ask for Alky's hand in marriage, but they delayed. When they finally allowed him over, they sat him near the door rather than inviting him in. Secretly they were hoping

Costas and Alky on the streets of Athens. Handwriting says, "How beautiful is the path of life together with you."

to dissuade the young couple's plans. Finally, lacking good reason to say no, they gave permission for the marriage. Soon they grew to love Costas as their own.

Alky's experience at Millar was similar to Costas's. The in-depth study of God's Word thrilled her soul, and a message by the same chapel speaker who had so moved Costas stirred her heart as well. But was her calling to be a missionary? The prospect frightened her. How could she leave her family in Greece? And how would she survive in a primitive environment?

During one summer break Alky became very sick, nearly dying. She felt the strength leaving her body, and she cried to the Lord, "If you give me my life, I'll go with Costas to the

Life in the Greek Army

mission field. Wherever You want me to go, Lord, I will go."

Eventually her health returned, and Alky took this as her own personal call. When Costas read her letter describing the experience, he was overjoyed. God was making their path clear.

After Alky's third year at Millar she returned to Athens, where she and Costas were married. She then returned to Canada to complete her studies, while Costas remained in Greece. Having fulfilled his obligatory military service, he was now deeply involved with a national youth ministry known as Κίνηση Ευαγγελικής Νεολαίας (KEN, Movement of Evangelical Youth).

Costas became well known as a charismatic leader among the evangelical churches throughout Greece. His father had given him a scooter, by which he traveled to youth meet-

Traveling by scooter to youth meetings throughout Greece

ings across the country. One Christmas he organized a surprise youth conference near Thessaloniki, to great success. This was a season of ministry preparation and training.

Costas applied to three mission societies. He received two routine replies, but the third—from a Mr. Vine of Regions Beyond Missionary Union (RBMU)—impressed him greatly. This mission had recently begun work with primitive tribes in Dutch New Guinea. Would Costas and Alky be interested?

Costas responded, and when Alky graduated from Millar in 1960, they were sure of their calling to New Guinea. They enrolled at the University of North Dakota for specialized training in field medicine and linguistics. Then it was off to RBMU headquarters in Philadelphia, Pennsylvania, where they lived while raising financial support.

Alky as a student at Millar

Over the next couple of years the couple traveled to every corner of North America, speaking in churches and homes about their future ministry. Slowly the support came in, and in April 1963 they waved goodbye to dear friends, holding their first child, Johnathan, born in Philadelphia six months earlier.

Costas and Alky could not know the trials and joys ahead. It was enough to obey, confident that the sovereign God who had called them to this adventure would walk with them every step.

But before we continue their story, we must wind time back eighteen years and gain some understanding of the world into which they were about to embark.

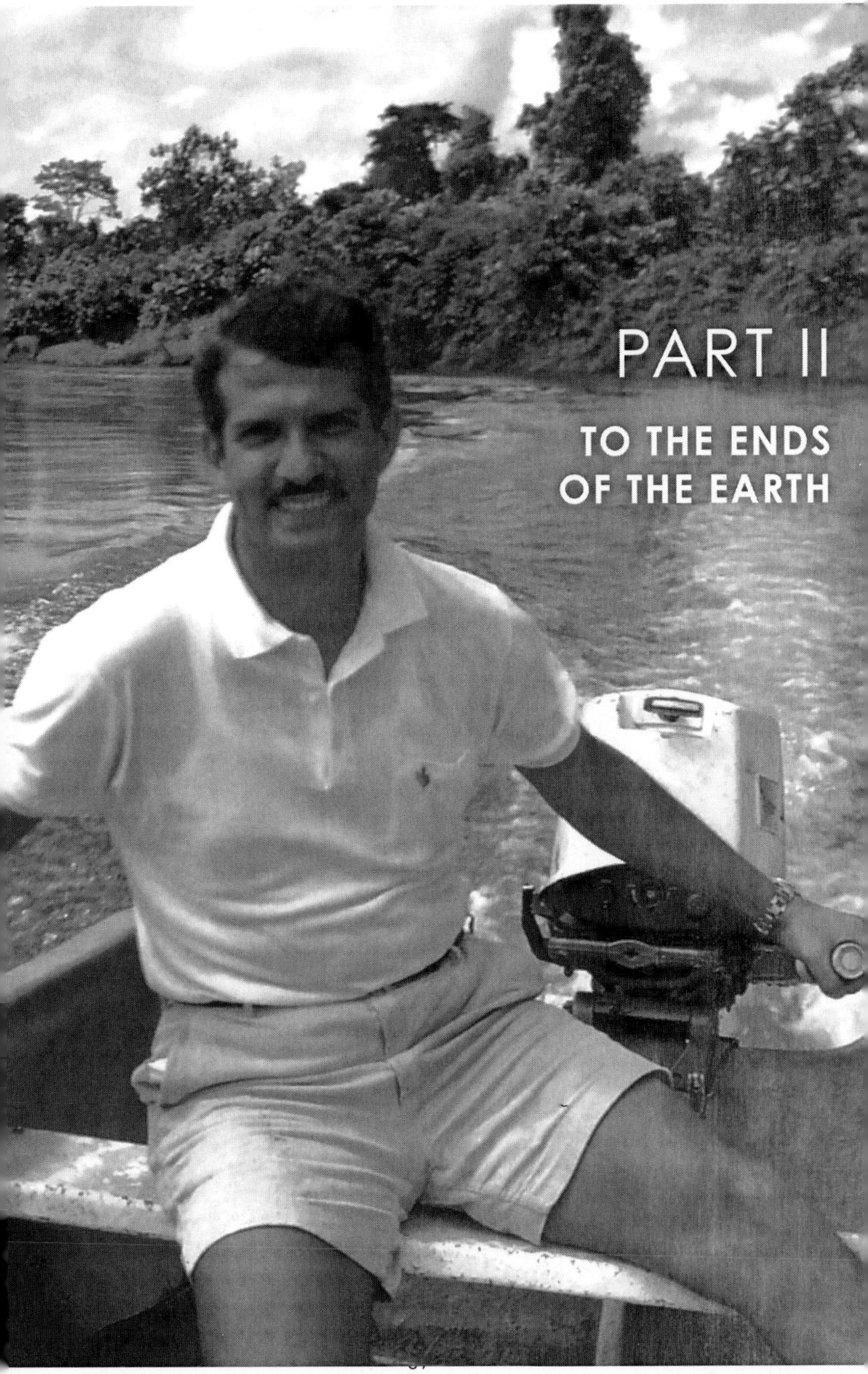

PART II

TO THE ENDS OF THE EARTH

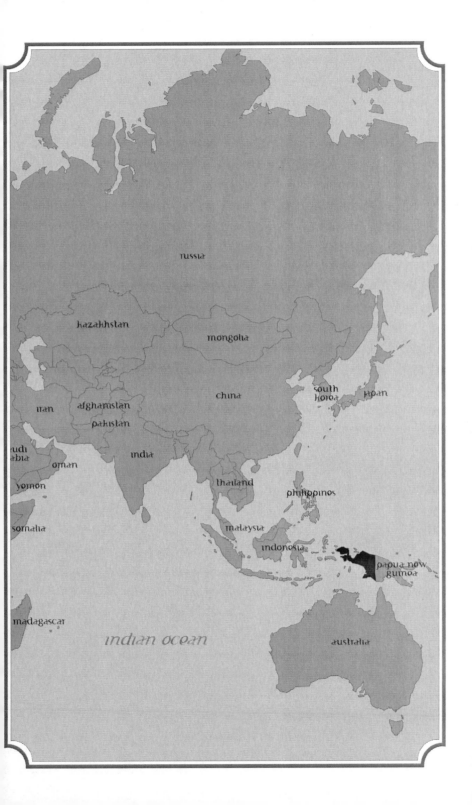

IRIAN JAYA

• Manokwari

• Minyambou

• Fak Fak

⊕ Airstrips built
by Costas Macris

⊕ RBMU stations

🏠 Macris family
residence

▨ Lakes Plains area

⛰ Mountains

〰 Rapids

N
W   E
S

CHAPTER 3

THE WORLD FINDS SHANGRI-LA

The *Gremlin Special,* a US Army C-47, lumbered noisily above dense jungle canopy, its Pratt and Whitney Twin-Wasp engines pummeling the air as it raced over uncharted valleys below. It was Sunday afternoon, May 13, 1945, and World War II was nearing its end. For the twenty-four American servicemen and women aboard, this sightseeing flight was a welcome break from the rigors of war. Ninety minutes earlier they'd lifted off in clear skies from Sentani base, New Guinea, the well-known headquarters for American General Douglas MacArthur, his South Pacific base of operations.

The *Gremlin's* pilots steered the stubby craft into an enormous valley and dropped altitude. The passengers gazed downward, noses and foreheads pressed against cold glass, straining to see the terrain.

"There's a village. With huts!"

"And look at the terraced fields."

An unexplored civilization spread out beneath. They'd heard that the interior of New Guinea, mostly uncharted, was inhabited by cannibalistic Stone Age tribes. Now they could tell friends back home they'd actually seen headhunters with their own eyes. No wonder these flights had become popular weekend excursions—modern man could witness a different world.

Tragically, quick-forming cloud cover caused the *Gremlin Special* to crash into a mountainside. Only three passengers survived, and for two months the world anxiously read descriptive accounts of the military's attempt to rescue them. With the aid of heroic paratroopers and steely-nerved glider pilots, the survivors were eventually saved, but not before their misfortune had introduced the world to the region's Stone Age inhabitants.

A BURDEN FOR PARADISE

During the weeks of rescue flyovers, an American navy airman named Paul Gesswein became familiar with the hidden tribes. During the hours in his aircraft seat far above the valley—dubbed Shangri-La by idealistic reporters—his interest outgrew mere cultural curiosity. He was a follower of Christ, and his conviction grew that these newly found tribes should hear the good news. *But how can they ever hear?* he wondered. *What will it take to share with them the love of Jesus?*

The war ended, and back on home soil Gesswein found his questions had morphed into full-on convictions. He knew his introduction to the lost tribes of the Hidden Valley was no accident. God was calling *him* to go back with the gospel. Unsure as to how this might happen, he took the first step, enrolling at Prairie Bible Institute, a small missionary training school isolated in the grasslands of Alberta, Canada. Energized by his study of the Bible, he delved into his classes with a passion, waiting for God to open the door to Dutch New Guinea.

The key to that door was provided three years later in the person of missionary recruiter and statesman Ebenezer Vine—a British pastor and businessman with an unquenchable zeal for world evangelization. During World War II he was voted general director of Regions Beyond Missionary Union[1]—an organization among the "grand old dames" of the modern missionary movement, founded in 1873 under the influence of such luminaries as China's Hudson Taylor and Africa's Dr. David Livingstone. The war now ended, England enjoyed a resurgence of missionary zeal. A fresh wave of young recruits volunteered to go to the ends of the earth. But going cost money, and the nation's impoverished churches had limited funds to meet the demand. The RBMU board sent Mr. Vine on a three-month recruiting and fundraising tour of North America. He would stay fifteen years.

Vine was an engaging character with a gift for bringing distant lands alive in his hearers' imagination. His set jaw, zeal, and disciplined yet gracious manner endeared him to the many Bible school and church groups to whom he spoke. He traveled tens of thousands of miles, crisscrossing the continent, challenging students to give their lives to that which mattered most. He unashamedly made known the needs and opportunities—and difficulties—that lay ahead for any who might join RBMU's pioneering work in India, Nepal, Congo, Peru, or Borneo.

When Ebenezer Vine finished his fall 1948 presentation at Prairie, Paul Gesswein rushed to his side. He excitedly shared his story, explaining his call to the inner highlands of Dutch New Guinea, then appealed with fervency to the senior statesman: Would RBMU help him get there?

The gray-haired leader gazed intently at the young man, recognizing Spirit-inspired resolve. Thoughtfully, he promised, "By God's grace, we will."

Vine took up the challenge, unaware the task would consume him for years. He began to inquire and soon learned that several mission agencies had tried to establish a postwar work in the New Guinea interior but had been turned down by the Dutch government, who couldn't guarantee safety to foreigners. Undaunted, Vine approached officials several times until finally he secured a meeting with a Dutch minister at the Hague. The door finally opened, and the small mission began actively planning to expand their work to the large island.

So it was that in early 1954 Gesswein and his new wife, Joy—along with Bill and Mary Widbin—set sail to the land of their calling. Nine years had passed since the Shangri-La flyovers. *Finally*, Paul thought when his feet again touched New Guinea soil. *Finally the dream is coming true.*

Ebenezer Vine surely felt that way as well. In his Bible, near Matthew 17, was later found the inscription, "November 2, 1950. New Guinea. Said to this mountain, 'Be thou removed in the name of Jesus.'"

By God's sovereign design, the stubborn mountain was beginning to budge.

A SHARED VISION

By the mid-1950s, others were dreaming of New Guinea as well. The Christian and Missionary Alliance (C&MA) and the Unevangelized Fields Mission (UFM) sent their own recruits, expanding on work begun before the war. Other organizations joined, and together they turned MacArthur's old Sentani base into a beachhead for a war of a different kind.

At first the groups experienced some territorial tension, but they soon forged an agreement for dividing the interior highlands. RBMU was allocated the Swart Valley, named for the Dutch explorer who had discovered it decades earlier.

Eleven-thousand-foot peaks pierced the sky, surrounding a lush panoply of dense jungle, cascading waterfalls, and tiny villages clinging tenaciously to razor-edged ridges. It was populated by the Dani tribe, steeped in tribal warfare, witchcraft, and cannibalism.

With considerable joy, the first RBMU airstrip and mission station in the central highlands was opened in June 1957 at Karubaga—a feat made possible by a vital sister agency, the Missionary Aviation Fellowship (MAF). Their sturdy fleet of small aircraft, flown by even sturdier pilots, paved the way, ferrying missionaries and cargo to the interior. MAF was a necessary lifeline, allowing the Karubaga-based work to progress with modern efficiency.

Karubaga was an ideal spot for this first continuous work with the Dani tribesmen, for the surrounding region was home to nearly twelve thousand souls. The late 1950s saw RBMU missionaries arriving in force. Buildings rose from the jungle, lining the new airstrip. Houses, sheds, and a sawmill took shape. Before long a small outpost had been scratched out of the harsh terrain.

New RBMU teammates had joined Gessweins and Widbins, many of them inspired by Ebenezer Vine's fruitful speaking tours. They included the Martins, the Richardsons, the Dekkers, the Dales, the Masters, Winnie Frost, and Judy (Neff) Eckles—hardy individuals with faith that God could do the impossible. Ebenezer Vine visited Karubaga in 1959, and upon his return to the States he spoke with even more zeal concerning the work in Dutch New Guinea. His words fell on ready soil, and through the early 1960s more men and women counted the cost and joined the RBMU team, including Bruno De Leeuw (and later his wife Marlys), the Clarkes, the Teeuwens, and the McCains.

God had planted a courageous, loving RBMU team at this remote jungle outpost—highly committed, faithful men and women, willing to sacrifice greatly for the evangelization of these unreached cannibalistic tribes. These servants would bear suffering and loss for the sake of the gospel. But they would soon witness one of the greatest evangelistic people movements in modern history.

THE SOIL GOD HAD TILLED

Long before RBMU's arrival, God had been preparing these isolated tribesmen for the dawning of gospel light. Their cultural beliefs held spiritual keys that would unlock their hearts to the message of Jesus.

C&MA missionaries had established initial contact with Dani and Danal tribes before World War II. They learned of the tribes' belief in *Hai*—a future millennial existence, hope in a great day of blessing, soon to be realized in their midst. In the early 1950s Catholic missionaries also approached these tribes, encouraging them to burn their fetishes in preparation for the *Hai* that Jesus would bring upon His return. Some of the tribesmen took this to heart and conducted a burning of fetishes in 1955. This prepared the way for more C&MA missionaries, and by the late 1950s many Danis began to turn from their animistic ways.

Into this context came the fledgling RBMU team, who found the people's hearts amazingly open to the gospel. In fact, a burgeoning movement was soon to explode. But this came with inherent dangers. Tribal peoples were known, sometimes, to "accept" Western teachings in order to gain material goods—the "cargo cult." The RBMU team was glad when tribes burned their fetishes and desired to turn from witchcraft, but one question loomed large: To what were they turning?

Burdened to see these tribes respond to the gospel, not just Western ways and customs, the team doubled down in teaching the Bible. They worked at making the gospel clear to these receptive peoples, spurred on by Mr. Vine's mandate: "Let us take to heart the basic fact that turning from tribal war, the burning of fetishes, or any other outward reformation, cannot become a substitute for inward change of heart."

Over time the gospel took hold in the Danis' hearts. Tribal elders and chiefs led the way, and soon feasts were established, during which villagers would throw their fetishes, occultic paraphernalia, and weapons of war into roaring flames. The missionaries spent days and weeks questioning the people, hoping to discern their true motives. They needed to go further and accept God's Son as the provision for their sin, trusting in His name. One local chief assured them of his understanding: "I am going to burn them because they are bad. I want to have eternal life. I want Jesus' blood to wash my heart. I want to go to heaven." The Spirit of God was at work! These people were receiving the truth of God's Word with joy.

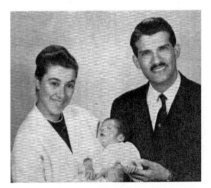

Alky and baby Johnathan before departing for Indonesia

Two more airstrips were carved into the mountain highlands, at Kanggime and at Mamit, and by 1960 new mission stations had been opened at both. The RBMU work was spreading, hundreds of Dani men and women responding to the gospel.

This was the setting when the young Greek couple, Costas and Alky Macris, with baby Johnathan, arrived in Dutch New Guinea. At long last—after years of preparation, prayer, and anticipation—their feet trod mission soil. It was April 17, 1963. The exciting journey had begun.

CHAPTER 4

KANGGIME, "THE PLACE OF DEATH"

The first thing Costas and Alky noticed about their new homeland was the wet, stifling heat. Alky first felt it in the Philippines as they changed planes en route. *My, how do these people make it?* she thought.

A new Boeing 707 carried them as far as the island of Biak, where they caught a boat to the main port of Jayapura. They were excited to meet their new teammates and naively hoped the whole RBMU team would greet them at the port. They felt some disappointment when only the field team leader met them. Later they would learn that travel from the interior to the coast was no small endeavor.

They flew to Karubaga, first on a large plane, then in a Cessna. Alky was terrified about flying in a small plane. But shortly before they were to board the Cessna, two young girls disembarked, laughing and smiling. *If they enjoyed the trip, then I can, too,* Alky resolved. During the flight she saw the pilot relaxed enough to read a book, and her fear subsided further. Of course, this was only the first of hundreds of flights she would experience over the next sixteen years—most of them in the smallest of planes.

As new team members, their first assignment was "station-sitting"—that is, caring for the work of veteran staff on furlough. Thus, after a short stay in Karubaga, they were flown to the highland station at Kanggime—which in Dani means "Place of Death"—where John and Helen Dekker had pioneered a new work.[2] The Dekkers would train the new couple for two months before traveling to North America for a year of furlough.

Costas and Alky had expected to live in a grass hut, but they were pleasantly surprised that the Dekkers had built a comfortable house, complete with a furnished living room, painted walls, and a cozy wood stove. For the transition period, John had built a small bush house the Macrises could call their own, made with round poles and split boards for siding, a floor of tree bark, and interior "wall paper" woven from reeds. The new accommodations came complete with a small outhouse, which Costas discovered lacked basic privacy, much to the interest of the curious local children.

The Macris home at Kaggime mission station

One of John's first tasks was to show Costas around the station. When John suggested they hike around the area,

Costas enthusiastically agreed, though he was wearing his city shoes; the family's belongings were still en route. Without much thought the two men set off on their hike. Up and down the hills they went, up one muddy path and down another, always careful to avoid the pig droppings, of course. They continued downward until they came to a river, crossed over small streams, then turned to make the strenuous climb back up to the Kanggime plateau. Costas's lowland lungs weren't prepared for the high altitude. And even though he slipped around without traction, he was careful not to complain, even when one of his shoe soles had to be tied with jungle vine. Only later did he refer to this trek as one of the most difficult he'd ever made.

The Macrises had heard about the Dani people—their new flock—and knew that many were accepting the Lord. The Danis, anticipating the new family's arrival to live in their midst, prepared a feast of wild pig and welcomed them with open arms. Exuberantly cheerful, the Danis lived up to their reputation as "the tribe that makes visitors feel like kings and queens since the gospel changed their hearts." In spite of forewarning, Costas and Alky needed time to become accustomed to the locals' lack of clothing and the wild appearance of many—bones through their noses and glistening, smelly pig grease rubbed on their skin. The Greek family was far from the streets of Athens!

Before leaving on furlough, the Dekkers introduced Costas and Alky to the difficult Dani language. Costas devoted himself to it fully and made quick progress. He was soon able to help with the literacy work among the Danis, and by mid-June the Macrises had taken over a large part of the program. They also gave out primers as people progressed through the course.

The Dekkers left on June 27 for ten months' furlough, leaving the Macrises, along with coworker Judy Neff, in charge of the station. As Costas watched the Dekkers' small plane lift off the runway, he felt overwhelmed, to the point of tears. When Alky saw his emotion, she asked, "Costas, what's wrong?" He replied, "Now all the responsibility for the people has fallen on me." Costas later admitted that if a second plane had been available, he might have left for home.

The discouragement passed, and soon Costas was hard at work. Among other assignments, John had left the young missionary with a difficult task—guiding the Danis in building a motorcycle trail between Kanggime and Karubaga, the main RBMU station. This was no small feat. Twenty miles of highland jungle and steep valleys lay between the two outposts. But the trail would considerably improve communication and movement of resources. Costas tackled his first big on-field challenge with delight.

Costas testing out the new bridge on the motor trail

With the help of hundreds of willing Dani workers, using only Stone Age tools and a few metal axes, the new missionary unleashed his creative and administrative efforts skillfully. After several months the road took shape, twisting up, over, and around the many ridges and valleys. The Dekkers returned to find the road nearly complete. Costas had even built a sturdy twenty-five-foot bridge across the largest gorge. John was impressed with the young man's perseverance.

The team's work had progressed in other ways as well. A new school building had been built, complete with hand-carved desks. Costas had constructed an outdoor amphitheater where villagers could gather for the teaching of God's Word. The literacy programs had progressed well. And decorative stone walls had been rebuilt around the Dekkers' home and clinic, surrounded by flower gardens bursting with lilies and rhododendrons. Apparently Costas had inherited a dose of his father's architectural skill. Judy recalls, "Helen and I thought we were smart, the way we had stone fences put up. Costas remade them, every stone fitting closely together." Judy also remembers Alky as a wonderful helpmate for the dynamic Costas. "He was the dynamite that got things moving, and she was the oil that kept them running smoothly."

Most important, the church had grown under Costas's leadership. Working closely with a strong Dani believer named Wununip, he had expanded the number of regional preaching locations from thirteen to twenty-four, and the youth work had grown. Costas and Alky had endeared themselves to the Dani people, and for years these new Dani friends went on to serve as able cowork-

Baby Johnathan making new friends in the highlands

ers in the evangelization of many yet-to-be-reached tribes.

It was at Kanggime, right from the start of his missionary career, that Costas's reputation for hard work and creative energy was forged amongst the RBMU team. To a lesser man the idea of station-sitting might mean maintaining the status quo; many were hesitant to build on another man's work. But this was foreign to Costas's thinking. Judy remembers,

"He didn't just station-sit when people were on furlough; he worked so hard both with the people and with the facilities on the station. Costas seemed to have boundless energy and did whatever he did with his whole heart and strength."

From the start, it was clear the jungles of Irian Jaya were a good fit for this young Greek dynamo. The challenges that lay ahead would test him time and again, but the Lord had created him equal to the task.

CHAPTER 5

THE MOVE TO NINIA

With the Dekkers' return came a new assignment for the Macris family, decided at the annual RBMU field conference of April 1964. The Macrises would now move to Ninia— in the Heluk Valley, east of Karubaga—to station-sit during Stan and Pat Dale's furlough. Ninia was higher in elevation than Kanggime—nearly six thousand feet, the highest of all RBMU stations. It was cold much of the time, and thick clouds often shrouded the area with a biting mist. The Dales, from Australia, had lived two years in this dark and difficult outpost.

The remote highland outpost of Ninia

This was home to peoples of the Yali tribe. Whereas the Danis had been generous in their acceptance of white-skinned foreigners, the Yalis were uninviting at best. Upon first contact, Stan and Canadian Bruno de Leeuw had spent eleven months carving an airstrip out of the rocky cliff-edged terrain. They'd hoped the Yali tribesmen would help with this endeavor, as the Danis had done in Karubaga and Kanggime. But the Yali attitude was markedly different. Their cool reception matched the gray climate. No jubilant greeting here, only wary uncertainty.

With the airstrip finished and in service, Stan had built a home for Pat and their four children. Ninia was a tough assignment even for this stalwart family. The valley was full of witchcraft, animism, and intertribal hostilities. The spiritual breakthrough seen among the Dani people seemed distant in every way. Yet the Dales and Bruno pressed forward tenaciously. They slowly made sense of the language and before long were able to carve the story of God out of the strange-sounding syllables.

After nearly eight months of hard work, the first small breakthrough came. A few women timidly approached Pat at her home. They listened intently to the simple yet culture-shaking stories of the Creator who sent His Son. Soon more women were gathering in Pat's kitchen, their thirst for truth overcoming their traditional shyness. The number grew to include men, and Stan was soon teaching God's Word daily to several hundred listeners. However, only a handful of the Yali professed any level of commitment, even though they recognized this strange teaching as liberating.

Opposition to the message—and the messengers—remained strong, especially among the powerful priest-leaders, who defended their ancient traditions. Nearly a third of the men had been initiated into rites of witchcraft, fetishes, and tribal warfare. To accept the intruders and their message would mean giving up their ancient ways, as well as much of their personal power. Some leaders were convinced the foreigners should be killed before their influence grew strong.

Others weren't so sure, afraid these white-skinned beings had come visiting from the afterlife. To kill them might unleash powerful spiritual forces against their people.

A Yali tribesman

This was the tense scenario when Costas and Alky arrived at Ninia. Costas flew in first, soon joined by Alky, two-year-old Johnathan, and their new baby, Haris. It was quiet, almost eerie, as they settled into the Dale's home. The station had been unoccupied for several weeks. Costas's first task was to make sure his family was comfortable in the dreary surroundings. He began to upgrade the Dales' unfinished home. Realizing he needed help, he radioed Kanggime, and soon a plane unloaded six hired Dani workers.

For several weeks Costas and his Dani friends refurbished the Dale house, making it well-insulated, suitable for his family's needs. He even installed an indoor water system with a toilet and shower. As at Kanggime, he built rock walls, flower beds, and stone-paved pathways. The Dales wouldn't recognize the place.

Costas then turned his full attention to the work for which they had established the station. A few of the Yalis were friendly, but most kept their distance. Then came an opportunity to show God's power over darkness: A tribal priest brought a dead pig and plopped it at Costas's door. Waiting for neither thanks nor payment, the priest scuttled away nervously. Costas didn't understand until a friendly tribesman explained. This pig had been killed by wild dogs. According to tribal belief, any human who ate the pig would immediately come under a curse and die. The Yalis were watching closely. Would their tribal spirits overcome these white invaders? Or did these foreigners possess a power greater than the darkness that ruled these valleys?

Once Costas understood, he turned to Alky. "Tonight we're eating pork!" And that's what they did, choosing to pray publicly to their Creator God before the meal, thanking Him for both food and protection. The next morning all of the Macrises were healthy and unharmed, to the surprise of their Yali observers. *What power do these beings possess that is greater than our spirits?* they wondered. Satan's stranglehold was beginning to loosen.

But the battle was just getting started. More "power encounters" were soon to follow, many of them dangerous. Years later Costas wrote, "During the early days there were difficulties untold. There were dangers, hardships, trials. . . . During that period I was nearly killed in two different incidents, once within viewing distance from our house, with Alky witnessing the scene!"

It was a day Alky would never forget. Several young men and boys had begun attending Costas's school, where they learned to read and write their own language. This angered one of the witch doctors. He fumed each day as the young males made their way down the mountain to this foreign intruder. Worse yet, his own boy was one of them! He forbade the students to continue their studies.

When Costas heard that the chief was hindering the students, he sent a message back to their fathers: "You tell those men, if anyone hinders you from coming to school, that person will have to deal with me!"

He wasn't exactly sure how he would follow through on his challenge, and he secretly hoped he wouldn't be tested. Alas, no such luck. The witch doctor persisted, and Costas knew he had to act. If he backed down, he would lose credibility.

Costas asked Alky's advice. She thought, then replied, "Well, you did say they'd have to deal with you if they didn't change their minds. I think you'd better go and deal with them." They both knew it was a dangerous move, but they sensed God's protection.

Alky watched as Costas, accompanied by the witch doctor's son, among other Yali men, and a few Dani workers, began the trek from the airstrip up to the mountain village. The path was narrow, and the group traveled single file, Costas leading. Where the trail dipped below the airstrip, Alky lost sight of the troupe, but they reappeared where the path rose.

The group neared the village, and suddenly a commotion broke out. Alky turned to her houseboy—a young Yali helper—and cried, "Pray! Pray!"

"Here I was, the missionary," she would later recount, "but I was asking this little boy to pray for me."

It was good that Alky was watching from a distance, unable to see the perilous turn of events. The witch doctor leapt onto a rock wall, then leveled his bow and drew his razor-sharp arrow back tight—*pointed directly at Costas's chest.*

"No, Father," cried the antagonist's son, jumping in front of Costas and pushing the surprised missionary out of the way. "Do not shoot this man! If you do, you'll have to kill me as well." The young man kept moving toward his father as he spoke, hoping to settle the matter peacefully. By now women were wailing, and tribesmen were screaming hostilities. To Alky below, it sounded like war.

"Get out of the way, Son. This man must die!" the father raged. The boy grabbed the weapon. Father and son struggled. The arrow released, its tip piercing the boy's ear as it sailed by his head. Blood spurted from the wound.

By now Alky had found binoculars and was observing

what she could, praying fervently for the group's safety. She saw pushing and shoving, and then something white being waved in the middle of the scene. To her it looked like hand-to-hand combat. Later she learned that Costas had taken off his white shirt and wrapped it around the boy's head to stop the bleeding.

The yelling subsided, but now other tribesmen had raised their arrows to finish what the witch doctor had started. Amazingly, the young Dani men with Costas were filled with boldness. They moved forward and grabbed the bows and arrows from the startled warriors, laying the weapons in a pile outside the village wall. Costas joined them, and soon all the village men were unarmed and, somehow, ready to listen.

Gently, through tears, Costas explained to these violent men why he'd come to their valley. "I don't want to hurt you. I want to serve you. All I ask is that you not threaten or harm these younger ones who desire to learn God's words." The missionary's air of authority, combined with his nonthreatening manner, engendered peace.

A short time later Alky saw Costas leading his group, single file, down the narrow mountain trail. When he reached the airstrip, Alky ran into his arms. Both were shaken but grateful. Costas didn't know if his actions had stirred up further trouble, and he slept little that night. Yes, God had spared his life, but had the public confrontation endangered his family?

The answer came at school hour the next morning. The young men and boys appeared, as usual. And with them came all the men and women from the village—*including the witch doctor*. Costas and Alky were overjoyed. From this point on, no one challenged Costas's right to teach their people. Many came regularly, including the witch doctor, who—later healed by God of an illness—professed himself a follower of Jesus.

A little later, Costas wrote,

After that recent opposition one of the boys came to me and said, "I want to come and live with the School Men in the School Village. It is so hard to live in the 'men's common house,' listening to the evil things. I am afraid if I stay there longer, I will also be evil! After I know more of the gospel and my heart grows stronger, then I will go and tell them about Jesus."

This is not the only boy who has expressed this desire. The Word is working, and we praise Him for His goodness. I thank Him, too, for enabling me to preach the Word and to see it work and bring fruit.

God was moving powerfully in the Heluk Valley. Now that interest was growing and trust was building, Costas intensified his efforts. He expanded the literacy program, and when their time at Ninia ended, seventy students filled the school. Three new preaching locations had been established away from the station. Blood, sweat, courage, and plain hard work had made this possible—not to mention powerful prayer and a mighty faith. The gospel was advancing, and the Macrises considered themselves privileged to build on the good foundation laid by Stan, Pat, and Bruno.

Costas's enthusiasm was contagious through the constant difficulties. He wrote to supporters, "We do not mind if it rains all day or if the clouds roll over us! We are happy here doing God's work while there is yet time. Let us take the challenges that God gives us with enthusiasm. Let us face them with the power of the Spirit. Then we will be happy in Him, and His presence will be sweet and real in our lives."

To add to the excitement, baby "Neil"—short for Cornelius—was born in October 1965. The family was now five. Costas and Alky delighted in their children and worked hard to provide a warm, safe environment for their young boys under austere circumstances. From the earliest age, the children were directly involved in the work—an expectation and privilege they would fulfill throughout their childhood and adolescent years. The home was strict, yet full of love; disciplinary, yet positive. Judy Eckles wrote, "Costas was a loving father. When he arrived at Kanggime, they only had Johnathan, and what a cutie he was. I remember Costas saying it was a relief to have a place of their own where they could discipline Johnathan as they pleased. He was never harsh."

To this day none of the Macris children would trade their jungle upbringing for a safer alternative elsewhere. Each believes sincerely they were honored to join in such a meaningful adventure. Yes, the dangers were real and the environment harsh, but the little family survived and thrived by Costas's tender strength and Alky's nurturing hand. Their parenting example has inspired many over the years.

In March 1966 the Dale family returned and marveled at the advancements in every direction. Their house was much improved, new buildings had been constructed, and the gospel and its fruit had spread across the valley. As at Kanggime, the young Macrises had proven effective teammates and expert station-sitters.

Costas and Alky were grateful to build on the work of fellow missionaries, especially while newly adjusting to the field. But after three years in Dutch New Guinea (recently renamed Irian Jaya), their hearts were hungry for a challenge they could call their own. Costas knew of hidden tribes yet to be reached with the good news, and he mapped out areas where he might establish a new station. In March 1965 he had expressed this desire at the annual RBMU field conference, while acknowledging that he and Alky were willing to go anywhere they were most needed. Costas described the response in a prayer letter shortly thereafter:

The more interesting item on the agenda . . . was "allocations." We were praying and were very anxious to see conference's decision regarding us for the coming year. And here it is! We will remain in Ninia until the Dales, the missionary couple responsible for this station, return from furlough. . . . Then we will move to Kamur, a south lowland station, so the Richardsons, the missionaries there, can be released to go on furlough.

Our utmost desire is to be used by God to the greatest end. We have yielded ourselves to Him, and our desire from day to day is to glorify the Lord. Although the door has not yet been opened to go to the unreached tribe in "area B," *we do not sit back disappointed.* The Lord has shown us from His Word that we should give thanks "*always* for all things unto God the Father in the Name of our Lord Jesus Christ."[3] So here we are in Ninia with a possible prospect to stay on if the missionaries of this station do not return. We take this challenge happily. We lift our hearts to God in praise, and then bend to the task He has given us with reverence and enthusiasm.

Despite their hearts' longing to start something new, Costas and Alky were content to station-sit for a third family. In dependence upon God and His sovereign plan they prepared to move to the south lowlands, where they would live among the treacherous people of Kamur.

CHAPTER 6

ON TO KAMUR

The highland tribes of the Danis and Yalis were not the only areas of interest to RBMU. In 1962 John and Glenna McCain had been sent to Kawem, a small outpost on the hot and swampy south coast of Dutch New Guinea. There they pioneered a work among the Roman Catholic-influenced Kayager people, in what was hardly a hospitable situation. Yet they persisted, and against all human odds a work of God was born in their midst.

Not far from the McCains, another new RBMU couple, Don and Carol Richardson, began a work with the Sawi people at a village named Kamur. These tribesmen knew little of the white men and their ways, but what they'd heard was positive. The foreigners offered tools that the swamp dwellers had never seen, implements that made life easier and hunting more productive. They were willing to let white men live in their village. *But who would want to live with us?* they wondered.

They had reason for their skepticism. The Sawi were a violent people. Like most jungle tribesmen, they valued strength, courage, and the arts of warfare passed down from their ancestors. But the Sawi supremely admired clever deception of an enemy by feigning friendship, only to betray and kill once trust had been established. Treachery was the ideal, summed up in their tribal saying, "To fatten with friendship for the slaughter." In fact, when Don told them the story of Jesus and His betrayer, Judas, the Sawi squealed in delight. "How cunning is that Judas?" They considered him the hero!

Richardson wrote of this in his popular book and film, *Peace Child,*[4] a gripping account of his experiences among the Sawis. The first few years were rough going; the people were receptive, but treachery and fighting continued, with no end in sight. Only when the Richardsons threatened to move to a different village of the same tribe, did the villagers make peace with their enemies. The morning following the Richardsons' ultimatum, the missionaries watched the official reconciliation, by way of a strange ritual. The two warring tribes stood facing each other. Women wailed shrilly, while a man broke from each line, and the two met in the middle. Each man carried a baby in his arms.

Don and Carol watched in amazement as the men exchanged the infants, reciting solemn vows of peace. The men then returned to their sides, each carrying the other's child. A roar of approval swelled up from both sides, barely drowning out the cries of anguish from each child's grieving mother. Each villager laid hands on that tribe's newest member, their "peace child." Then they mingled with their former enemies and exchanged gifts and greetings. The ceremony ensured that, as long as each child lived, neither tribe would bring violence to the other.

This was the breakthrough Don and Carol had prayed for. Not only did it stop the bloodshed, but by God's sovereign design it provided a beautiful redemptive analogy by which to explain the gospel. Don told them, "Jesus is God's peace child, given so we might live in peace with God." The message stuck, and before long a few tribal leaders invited this divine Peace Child into their hearts, and a fledgling church was born. True peace had visited the cannibals of Kamur.

THE MACRISES AT KAMUR

In April 1966 a small floatplane buzzed low over thick jungle and sago swamps, set-
tling ever lower until its floats cut furrows into a brown serpentine river. The craft beached itself against the muddy shore, and Costas, Alky, and their three boys stepped off the plane onto dry land and into their next assignment.

On the river at Kamur

Job number one was to build a temporary house, which Costas accomplished quickly with the help of local tribesmen. Costas wrote to supporters,

> Only last week I finished the stairs to the temporary house I built in Kamur. We just moved into it the other day, and we like it very much. It took three weeks to build it, but there is still much to do, especially as we want to keep out all the uninvited living creatures (snakes, bugs of all kinds, mosquitoes, etc.). We killed a very poisonous snake only thirty feet away from the house already! . . . This was in a busy part of the yard!

The river often overflowed its banks, requiring dirt walls built around the yard and home. Costas wrote, "A few days ago we looked out of the window in the morning and felt we were by ourselves in a boat house. There was water all around the house. The children, though, don't mind this. They just

The Macris home in Kamur

love the muck! . . . Poor Alky!"

With the Richardsons gone on furlough, Costas expanded his to-do list. He first cleared the jungle around the station to make room for a new school. The large building would provide space for both study and worship. He supervised the digging of a channel between their river and another river farther north—a project Don had started. The channel would provide better canoe access to nearby Sawi villages. And with characteristic flair, Costas made practical and cosmetic improvements to the Richardsons' house and yard.

Costas and Alky tenaciously built upon every aspect of the good work the Richardsons had started. What excited them most, though, was the Sawis' growing interest in the gospel. Villagers asked Costas and Alky to linger after nearly every Sunday service to explain how to receive Christ. Costas was thrilled at the people's response and wrote,

> The work here is progressing quite well. I preach the gospel in four different places each Sunday. Alky teaches the women here. I've started clinic work in three other villages. A number of young people are showing increased interest. School work has expanded to two new villages, and we are soon to start regular school in two more. Our work is scattered . . . and it seems that we keep busy all the time without being able to accomplish all we feel God will be pleased to do here.

As advancements progressed, so came the battle. The "peace child" ceremony had secured a truce between the two closest villages, but battles between others continued. Costas and Alky often felt overwhelmed by circumstances that would send those of lesser courage flying back home. As Costas explained,

Anything that could happen in any wild jungle village anywhere in the world could certainly take place here. For one thing, in our short stay here we have already had plenty of exciting experiences to write a book or two. A few snakes killed right in our yard. A battle with bows and arrows only thirty yards from our house. Constant strife that has often reached the point of breaking into violence. And only just four hours ago, I witnessed the battle in which three men were seriously wounded. One has a piece of a spear eight inches long in his back! And another was hit through the chest only an inch from his heart, with the spear going right through his chest and out his back!

We gave antibiotics—that was the only thing we could do. At least one man, we fear, will not survive his injuries. It is a long story of cruelty that goes back as far as the memory of these people, and of course as old as sin itself, ever since the devil established his domain in these swamps.

Sorrow . . . Agony . . . Fear . . . Cruelty . . . Pain . . . Suffering and despair! This is the package of sorrow that the devil has offered them, and they cling to it as a treasure until the day of their doom. Why? Oh, why should people in this world be so blind to the deceitfulness of the devil? Why should they reject the precious gospel of love, peace, and hope?

It wasn't only tribal warfare that threatened the Macrises and the work at Kamur. Many Roman Catholics in the region were hostile to RBMU. Once the police chief from a neighboring area, sympathetic to the Catholic cause, sent three men to the tribe where John and Glenna McCain were stationed. The policemen singled out Protestants and proceeded to burn their homes, chop up their canoes, and abuse their wives. The message was clear, and it spread throughout the region: Anyone who dared follow the Protestant missionaries could expect similar treatment! Also, Catholic school teachers were placed in neighboring tribes in order to exert their influence.

In spite of the threats, Costas pressed forward undeterred, writing after the police intimidation,

> A few of the heathen here who are unfriendly toward us got a little encouraged, thinking—I suppose—they could practice their old art and get away with it, since they would be on the police's side. I tell you there is nothing more dangerous in the jungle than a semi-civilized man without God. We prayed and sought guidance and protection from God, and kept on with our work.

Eventually senior police officials were notified, and the threats subsided, at least for a season. But tensions remained, with troublemakers creating hostilities wherever possible.

VICTORIES AND BREAKTHROUGHS

In spring 1967, just before the Richardsons' return, Costas wrote ecstatically about the spiritual progress they were seeing in a neighboring village:

> Our greatest joy is the beginning of what could become a break in the village of Hainam. Nearly all the response to the gospel message has thus far come from the village of Kamur; from Hainam we have found great resistance and extreme indifference.
> We wrote to friends before to pray for that village, which seemed to be such a stronghold of the enemy. Now, on Sundays many people from Hainam make special trips

to the station from their jungle homes to attend the gospel meetings. Also the boys and girls whom they would not allow to come to school started attending classes more regularly, and a number of women are attending our women's school. Recently, too, we had the joy of leading three people from there to the Lord. A number of young people are close to accepting the Lord. So join us in praising God. Hallelujah!

Many Sawi villagers began to turn explicitly from witchcraft and warfare. Some broke their weapons and fetishes and threw them in the river. Others burned them in large fires.

The Sawi literacy programs were expanding as well. During the Macrises' year in Kamur, school attendance increased fivefold. When students finished the basic course, they were moved to advanced classes. Many attended from a distance, so Costas constructed a School Village where advanced students lived together. It soon became a place of spiritual shelter and Christian discipleship. Costas was thrilled with the progress he saw among the young men. He wrote:

> The first phase of this project is finished, and nineteen young men with a good Christian testimony have moved in. Some of these young men already help us in the lifting of the burden of the spiritual ministry and have carried out both the teaching and preaching ministry successfully. . . . So we trust that the Lord will raise from among them the Christian leaders to lead His church.

BAD NEWS FROM NINIA

Even as they enjoyed spiritual successes in Kamur, Costas and Alky received shocking news from Ninia. Two young Yali believers—men whom Stan Dale had led to Christ and discipled—had been martyred while preaching in a distant valley.

Stan led a police contingent into that valley in search of the murderers, but they were ambushed, and Stan was struck by six arrows—one in his abdomen and another in his chest.

Stan survived and, by sheer force of will, trekked most of the way back to Ninia. Barely alive, he was flown to Karubaga for immediate surgery. He nearly died on the table, but eventually his body strengthened, and the indomitable Stan Dale ended up back on his feet. After weeks of recuperation, Stan and Pat returned to Ninia, embraced by the small, growing group of Yali converts. These new believers were shaken by the loss of their two friends, but Stan's determination fanned the flames of their trust in God. Their faith was being tested and was growing ever deeper.

Not long after the Dales' return, Costas wrote,

> I had the joy of going back to our precious station of Ninia to help with the first Christian baptism and the establishment of the first church. . . . Stan Dale, standing there in the water with his multiple scars from the six arrows that were embedded in his body and the extensive surgery done on him, pointed to his wounds and said, "Costas, it was worth it." And surely it was! Eighteen men and women went to the service, but there were many tears, as the absence of our beloved young men . . . was very real. These first martyrs of the church are in the presence of the Lord, whom they loved and for whom they gave their lives.

A CHAPTER CLOSES

Don and Carol Richardson returned from furlough to find their work and facilities in excellent condition. Don would later write,

> With remarkable selflessness, Costas and Alky volun-

teered to delay the beginning of their own pioneer ministry for still another year, in order that young Sawi "babes in Christ" might have constant spiritual nurture during the crucial early years of their Christian experience.

One year later, Carol and I returned from furlough to find, as Stan and Pat had found at Ninia, that more tribesmen knew Christ as Savior. Three new schools overflowed with hundreds of eager literates. The sick had been faithfully treated. Our own house and yard were greatly improved. And bouquets of flowers welcomed us in every room!

We looked around us in awe. Never had we seen the Spirit of Christ more exuberantly displayed than we saw it in dear Costas and Alky! Though they had greatly improved our home, they themselves had lived the year in an even smaller and less convenient structure.

The Macrises had enjoyed a profitable year—in fact, four profitable years. From Kanggime to Ninia, and then south to Kamur, they had faithfully and noticeably advanced the work of each station. Still their hearts yearned for a pioneer work of their own. The answer came during field conference in March 1967, about which Costas reported,

> We were presented with the greatest challenge of our life! The area known as the Lakes Plains, which we recently surveyed, was given to us to evangelize. We were allocated there upon our return from furlough. We have lots of desires in our hearts, but the one most prominent is that the *lost* (and deprived for centuries) tribespeople of that lonely and isolated region will come to hear the message of salvation. This is an immense task ahead of us—a life ministry. It will take all we can give to the utmost—and even that the Lord might require—but our hearts are set to serve Him, and He has given us His joy.

But first they returned to Greece and North America to visit family, friends, and supporters on their first furlough. They had much to tell, for God had not only used *them*, but also those who'd supported them with prayer and donations. They packed their bags, put their household goods in storage, and headed to Athens in July 1967. What a joy to see family again. Johnathan was five, and with great pride he introduced Haris and Neil to grandmas and grandpas. How strange the bustling Athens streets must

Coworker David Martin and Costas studying a map of the Lakes Plains region

have seemed to these three little jungle monkeys! Where were the canoes? Why did everyone have light skin? And why did people wear so many clothes?

Many Greek believers had followed the family's journeys from afar and were interested to hear the Macrises' stories firsthand. Curious crowds—including some Orthodox Christians—packed the evangelical churches where they spoke. With characteristic zeal Costas used these meetings to preach the gospel. He traveled to many areas of Greece and spoke nearly every evening to large gatherings. This was a season of fruitful ministry.

After two months in Greece the family left little Neil with grandparents and boarded a plane for North America—first to the States, then to Canada. Costas and Alky shared enthusiastically about the work in Kanggime, Ninia, and Kamur. They told of the amazing moving of God among the Dani tribes, of learning strange languages, and of being faced with bows and arrows and angry witch doctors. They told of Stan Dale's courage and brush with death, and of the recent baptisms in

Ninia. Always they emphasized God's triumph in every circumstance and how He had prepared and sustained them to shine His light in one of the world's darkest domains.

Then they shared their dream . . . the dream that had been growing for several years, the desire to pioneer a work of their own in a new place, truly a region beyond. The Lakes Plains area was calling, so they shared their burden openly, pleading with supporters and friends for a fresh covering of prayer.

By April 1968 they had traveled thousands of miles and spoken at meeting after meeting. They returned to Greece, tired but ready to return to their adopted homeland—Irian Jaya.

Saying goodbye to family—especially parents and grandparents—was never easy, but the calling in their hearts was certain. The adventure of their lives lay ahead; the unreached tribes of the Lakes Plains were waiting for the gospel of Jesus Christ.

CHAPTER 7

A SEASON TO PREPARE

Explorer Matthew Stirling leaned forward in his canoe, scanning the river ahead. The dull roar of cascading water grew ever louder as the Dayak tribesmen surrounding him strained their oars against the rapid current.

As expedition leader, he had done his research. He knew this stretch of the mighty Mamberamo River would be dangerous. Watching the skill of the oarsmen, however, set him at ease. Their fluency as canoe men was reassuring. He praised the day he had the sense to hire them for this trip, from their native Borneo.

It was July 15, 1926. The "Stirling Expedition"[5] was slowly fighting its way into the vast, little-explored interior of Dutch New Guinea. A joint Dutch-American enterprise, the company of over four hundred men was made up of 75 Ambonese soldiers, 130 expert Dayak canoers, and 250 Indian convicts conscripted as porters. Their highway was the Mamberamo, a confluence of mountain runoff and marshy silt. Fed by glaciers on the central Snow Mountains, this massive waterway is the widest river in all Indonesia.

The expedition's objective was clear: to explore and map this vast, unknown region that lay south of the Pacific Ocean and north of the Snow Mountains. From a wide delta at its mouth, the river was easily navigated for the first hundred miles. Once the expedition encountered the beginnings of the van Rees Mountains, however, they braced for seventy-five miles of treacherous rapids.

Stirling had earlier described the rapids in his diary,

> Shooting the Edi and Marine Falls en route . . . report the trip the thrill of a lifetime. Dashing over four and five foot falls in the water; sinking into depressions, which hide the canoe from sight; or skating sidewise off from great boiling mounds of water forced up by a tremendous force from below; skirting between great whirlpools which could suck down a canoe like a straw; rocking on curling waves like the sea; slipping between ragged rocks—all at express speed.[6]

If not for the skill of the Dayak canoers, Stirling would later write, their fate would have been a watery grave. Eighteen years earlier another expedition had attempted the rapids, only to lose sixteen men, tossed and then held submerged by giant foaming whirls.

Stirling and company labored ahead, at times required to carry their canoes around boulders in the river. At last, having conquered the rapids, they found themselves in a region known as the Lakes Plains. The mountains quickly leveled away, the land now flat as Kansas. And the mighty Mamberamo, instead of tumbling in a rush to the sea, coiled lazily under a hot tropical sun. The water became murky, all marsh and mosquitos.

Stirling pressed ahead with a small party, drawing maps

and encountering tribes and villages. Months later the expedition would make its way back to the Pacific, having successfully explored the region, untouched by modern civilization.

A NEW EXPLORATION

Fast-forward forty-two years. Alky Macris had heard about the treacherous Mamberamo rapids. When Costas first began dreaming toward the Lakes Plains, she joined in his enthusiasm. She knew he had been yearning to open a new station. They had been delighted to care for and build upon the work of their fellow missionaries, but they both knew it was time to spearhead a new venture.

As their plans solidified, it became clear that trekking into the Lakes Plains meant following Stirling's path, which led right through those tumultuous rapids—a prospect that unsettled Alky. A woman of unusual faith, she had seen the Lord deliver Costas from several near-death encounters with tribal warriors. She had taken her children to one of the most remote jungles on earth and had experienced God's protection and answered prayer time and time again. But for some reason a fear about Costas facing those deadly rapids settled upon her soul like a chilling mist. She began to dread the day of his departure, fearful she would lose her husband.

Missionaries are not immune to fear and depression. Perhaps they are more prone to emotional trauma due to the circumstances of their work and the demands upon their psyches. The apostle Paul, arguably the greatest missionary of the early church, admitted to fear, despair, and feelings of hopelessness. Jesus Himself—our perfect example—anticipating the cross while in Gethsemane, cried out in anguish. In some circles—especially among those in full-time ministry—it may be fashionable to hide behind a cloak of invincibility, but each of us must come to terms with our true, full measure of weakness. The Macrises were no exceptions.

During the family's furlough year, the rapids had weighed heavily on Alky's mind. She remembers her anxiety and depression while visiting supporters in British Columbia. She was concerned for little Haris, who, at two years old, was not eating well. On top of this, Costas had to be gone from the family for extended visits to various parts of North America. These family challenges, combined with fear of the future in general, and the rapids and their new assignment in particular, loomed like giant suffocating shadows, threatening to strangle all the faith she could muster. Yet she pressed ahead faithfully, choosing confidence that the God who had led and protected them during their first term would remain equally present during their second.

If Costas was intimidated, his prayer letters didn't show it. He planned exuberantly for their new venture, his enthusiasm contagious as he shared the vision. Aware that any long-term presence in the Lakes Plains would require a boat, he made known his need for a vessel that would not only carry him into the region, but also provide a base of operations while he carved a house out of the jungle. His joy knew no bounds when Greek believers joined together and raised funds for a beautiful, new eighteen-foot cabin cruiser, with a fourteen-foot skiff to be pulled behind. It was a wonderful confirmation that God's hand was with them.

Just before returning to Irian, Costas received word that, by arrangement of a dear friend, the boats and a trailer had been crated and shipped from Rotterdam and Antwerp. They were to arrive in late April by British ship at the West Irian port of Sukarnapura.

The wonderful thing about all this [he wrote] is that everything is paid thus far. We will only have to pay as yet the customs, handling, shipping, and insurance charges. But who worries about that? The boats are bought and paid for. This fulfillment of God's will has involved *you* as well as us. We took this step of faith together, and we now rejoice together at its fulfillment. What to some seemed, a few months ago, an impossible dream is already a reality. Now we want to press on until the boat is through customs and inside the Lakes Plains, making the establishment of a witness possible among those primitive tribespeople.

In a subsequent letter, Costas laid out the basic plan for his upcoming journey:

First, we have to sail into the ocean, after that in the torrents of the River Mamberamo, still after, the difficult passage of the waterfalls, and finally the long trip in our effort to reach the village Taburtua, where we are going to make our temporary station. From the village Taburtua we shall go backwards to the small affluence of the river, where the Kwijon tribe lives. [Costas here used the Dani term for these people, who actually called themselves Taori.] Pray that the Lord will guide us to the suitable place for the settlement of our permanent station and the construction of an airstrip.

The Macrises arrived back in Irian Jaya in mid-July, and soon the boats cleared customs, and they completed preparations. Costas planned to make the dangerous trip alone, leaving Alky and the boys in Sentani until he established a beachhead in the jungle. Then came a welcome surprise: Fellow missionary John McCain volunteered to accompany Costas until he safely passed the rapids. John's companionship was a welcome gift, but his skill on the water would be of even greater value; he had grown up on the waterways of Louisiana and was an expert boatman. Costas expressed his relief and gratitude:

God sent a great help. One of our fellow missionaries, John McCain, who is very experienced in many fields, volunteered to come with me on this dangerous trip. His wife was very sick and for six months had to lie on her back in a hospital in Australia. The Lord spared her life, and they had just returned to the field, so John was able to come with me, and *I did not have to go alone.*

CHAPTER 8

RIDING THE RAPIDS

Costas kissed Alky and his boys goodbye, unsure when he would see their sweet faces again. It was the evening of August 9, 1968. He and John slept on the boat that night and set out to sea at 4:15a.m. The Mamberamo River mouth, their entrance to the Lakes Plains, lay 225 miles west by open sea. They made better time by traveling separately, John in the little skiff with its twenty-horsepower outboard motor and Costas in the larger cabin cruiser, which they had christened the *Good News*. At the end of the first day they found a secluded beach on a small island off the coast, where they tied up the boats and made camp.

After two days they reached the mouth of the mighty river. They turned south and crossed the tumultuous water where river and ocean met. The journey upriver had begun. Anticipating their need for extra fuel, the men had arranged for MAF pilots to drop supplies along the way. Pilot Bob

Brueker wrote in a letter to his parents,

> Late yesterday afternoon I flew up along the coast, west
> to the little village (four or five huts) of Sasakar, about
> one hundred miles from Sentani. We dropped them
> fourteen jerry cans of fuel. Melvin Isaac went along,
> and he pushed the cans out as we made low passes over
> the beach. Latest word today is that they have made it
> to the mouth of the river. Costas has his heart in this
> and is determined to reach those people. The other
> day he said, "There has been so much time and money
> spent getting the boat ready and everything else, but to
> know that those people will be able to hear the gospel
> makes it worth everything!"

The river's current began to strain the motors. The further
upstream they went, the stronger the flow. But after nearly
one hundred miles, they arrived just below the rapids. They
beached and waited for Don Beiter to land his MAF floatplane nearby on the river. Don remembers the experience
clearly:

> The rendezvous was at the base of the rapids, about
> eighty air miles inland. There is a smaller range of
> mountains that separates the central swamp from the
> ocean. The large Mamberamo River penetrates this
> range through a narrow gorge that created a major rap-
> ids obstacle. For the boat to safely navigate the rapids
> and gorge, I landed in the river, meeting with the boat.
> There, cargo from the boat was put into the floatplane
> to lighten the boat for its trip through the swift current
> of the rapids. With a watchful eye I circled overhead
> while the boat proceeded through the rapids and the
> gorge uneventfully.

What may have appeared uneventful from above was less
so at water level. At one point the bow of Costas's boat was
sucked downward into a vortex. He immediately slammed

the throttle forward, causing the engine to scream until the whirlpool released its grasp. Natives would later tell Costas of several motorized canoes that had recently traveled the same route. The boats and their occupants were swallowed completely by a similar whirlpool, only to resurface a week later in the exact same spot.

Costas pushed forward cautiously. He knew that boulders lay hidden beneath the river's churning surface. Later he would write about the danger he sensed as they traversed the narrow gorge:

Costas's boat approaching the dreaded rapids, as seen from the air

> The hand of the Lord was strong. Three times He saved our lives from certain death! . . . While going through the rushing waters of a series of rapids, a huge log hit us and just about stalled the engine. Then, just five miles above the rapids, our outdrive was put out of action because of the log that had hit us. We were now in calm waters and knew that God wanted to show us that it was He *alone* who saw us through.

At long last the dreaded rapids were behind them. Don landed the floatplane near the boats, and fuel and provisions were quickly reloaded. The plane departed and returned the following day, August 15, ferrying in a Dani boy who had served as one of Costas's workers since Kanggime. The boy would continue upriver with Costas, replacing John so he

Above the rapids, reloading provisions from plane to the boat Good News

could return to help care for his wife.

Back in Sentani an anxious Alky waited for news, praying for a good report. Gene Newman, an MAF accountant, walked to her house from his nearby office, carrying the message she'd hoped to hear. MAF radio traffic had confirmed that Costas had passed through the rapids safely! Overcome with relief, she thanked God. Once again He had spared Costas's life from imminent danger.

A JUNGLE FOOTHOLD

Safely above the rapids, supplies reloaded, Costas watched the floatplane speed over the river's surface, take off, then angle back toward the coast, the drone of its engine gently giving way to the jungle sounds. Anxious to get moving, Costas started the inboard engine and nudged the *Good News* out into the current, heading upriver. By a straight line on his map, the Lakes Plains region was only thirty miles away. But the river's twists and turns made the journey a hundred miles by water.

For several days Costas and his young helper pushed forward, until finally they arrived at the region of which Costas had dreamt for so long. They scouted two rivers off the Mamberamo, looking for ground high enough to escape the frequent flooding. Both rivers eventually narrowed and turned into swamps, where trees and vines forced a return to the main channel. Travel was slow. Costas possessed a basic map of the area, but the flat, winding rivers had changed course often, making the map nearly obsolete.

At one point, while on the water, Costas thought he heard the voice of someone speaking the Dani language from around the next bend. He blamed his imagination until suddenly a canoe appeared, carrying a Dani believer Costas knew from Kanggime. This man had felt the Lord prompting him to travel down to the Lakes Plains, unannounced, to find Costas and help him begin his work. Costas couldn't believe it! He praised God for this unexpected encouragement.

On the fourth day the small group arrived where the main river branched into two tributaries, the Rouffaer and the Idenburg. Here Costas clearly sensed the Lord telling him in his spirit, *This is the place.* At first glance the location was nothing special—no remarkable features, the ground apparently no higher than other spots they'd considered. But because of this inner prompting Costas pulled to shore, jumped out of the boat, and surveyed the area. He began to envision how a station could be built in this jungle location—a long airstrip over there, a home for his growing family here, a clinic, a school . . .

Initial days of clearing land at Taiyeve

He felt confirmation in his spirit. *Yes*, he prayed as he fell asleep that evening aboard the boat, *This is the spot. Thank you, Lord, for guiding me.* In the coming years he would often praise God for His perfect direction. This proved to be the only area in the region that didn't suffer severe annual flooding, and the perfect spot for an airstrip. He named the new station Taiyeve, after the local tribe.

Fellow missionary Jacques Teeuwen would later write,

> I remember asking Costas why, out of dozens of other possibilities, he had chosen this particular spot. "Because the Lord told me," Costas answered simply. I just smiled. It could not have been that simple. When the rainy season started, all surrounding areas were flooded. Taiyeve and its newly built airstrip remained dry, except for a few meters at the bottom of the strip.

On August 31 Costas wrote the following to some dear friends in St. Louis:

> Hallelujah! Glory to God! I am here at this place I prayed and planned and worked to get to! The amazing thing is that I am here alive and unhurt even while going through big ocean storms . . . even though I came through hundreds of miles of swirling rivers, even though I had to literally climb up the treacherous rapids of the Mamberamo River.

Even more exciting, Costas was able to make contact with several men who belonged to the Taiyeve tribe, who were overjoyed to receive this new visitor and forge a relationship. The Taiyeve had been trading partners with the highland tribes for years. They had noticed the positive influence that white-skinned missionaries had brought to the Danis—the cessation of hostilities, the useful tools and other goods. Word had arrived from the highlands that Costas was coming to the Lakes Plains, so the Taiyeve were anxious to greet him.

Lakes Plains tribes were nomadic, constantly moving wherever fishing and hunting could sustain them. Thousands of tribesman were scattered, hidden throughout the region, and Costas knew their nomadic lifestyle was detrimental to their well-being. He decided to create central settlements where the Taiyeve and others could gather for medical treatment, education for their children, and spiritual instruction. Only in gathered communities could churches be planted and the gospel bring lasting change to the tribes throughout the region.

Costas and his helpers immediately began to hack away at the jungle, clearing an airstrip. After each day's work he would return to the cabin cruiser to draft plans for the new station. When twenty Dani workers hiked down from the highlands in order to help, the work advanced even faster. Don

First contact with the tribesmen of Taiyeve

Beiter flew many trips to support the effort, initially bringing tools—axes, machetes, shovels, pickaxes, saws, carpentry tools, nails—as well as rice and other food staples for the workers. Over the next several months Don made thirty-eight flights from Sentani to Taiyeve, carrying average loads of six hundred pounds—a total of nearly eleven tons of material and personnel. He remembers, "All of the work was done by hand. The location was totally jungle, tall trees seventy feet tall or more, with jungle vines entwining everywhere. As the weeks went by, each trip flying there I noticed more land cleared and ditching started for airstrip drainage."

Land was also cleared for gardens, planted with vegetables to feed the workers. Before long Costas began work on a house, which he hoped to finish before his family would join him mid-December.

Costas was pleased. He had arrived safely upriver, and he had established a solid foothold at their new home. Yet days of sorrow lay just ahead, days that would challenge the RBMU staff to their core.

CHAPTER 9

THE SENG VALLEY TRAGEDY

The missionary community relied heavily on the day's technology—the single sideband radio network. These small radio handsets allowed missionaries in West Irian and in neighboring Papua New Guinea to stay in daily contact with teammates throughout the region. The radio was often a means by which isolated families received comforting news and information from far across the island, and a way to call in needed planes and provisions. On rare occasions, however, the radio brought shattering news, conveying loss and heartache that affected the entire missionary community.

One fateful day the sideband crackled with the worst news imaginable. On September 25, 1968, RBMU's Stan Dale and Philip Masters had been attacked by hostiles in the Seng Valley and were presumed—later confirmed—dead. Accompanied by three Dani carriers, they had been trekking between the Dales' station at Ninia and the Masters' station at Korupun.

For several days their small party had been followed by a band of Yali warriors from Wikbun, a village in the north of the Seng Valley, near Korupun. The missionaries at last confronted the band, hoping to make known their friendly intentions but to no avail. The warriors surrounded Dale and Masters and killed them in a barrage of arrows. Two Dani carriers escaped with their lives and brought news of the attack to the outside world. Another Dani apparently died from altitude exposure while trying to escape over the mountains.

Both Dale and Masters had been burdened to take the gospel to this remote and hostile area. Legend said the Yalis of the Seng Valley were superior in witchcraft to the Danis. They were known to be cunning and hateful, determined that no white-skinned invaders would diminish their power and destroy their time-honored ways. Someone had once warned Stan, "Don't go into the Seng. That's where Satan's seat is."

Despite the warning, the courageous men felt compelled to make contact with these hostile warrior tribes. Sometime prior, Stan had written a sober plea to supporters in Australia: "Please continue to remember us in prayer. Unfortunately, there is not much interest in places where visible results are small. We trust that something will be done in our areas to bring glory to God, even though we may be unknown." Prayers for the Seng Valley would be answered, but in a way no one could have predicted or desired.

A terse telegram reached RBMU's Philadelphia headquarters: "PHIL AND STAN MISSING ON TREK. BELIEVED KILLED. SEARCH IN PROGRESS. 9/30/68 a.m." Immediately search parties were sent to verify everyone's fears. MAF pilots and a geological survey helicopter braved stormy weather, until they finally came upon the rocky creek shore, the site of the massacre. Hundreds of arrows lay scattered across the creek bed, bits of bone and dried blood confirming the men's deaths. The searchers returned to base heavy hearted.

"Oh, Lord," cried the bereaved teammates, "surely our friends didn't die in vain. But how can any good come from a tragedy like this?"

The two men's families—in fact, the island's entire missionary community—suffered and grieved. This vividly reminded Costas and Alky of the dangers they faced daily. Alky felt a bit guilty when she thought of her dear friends, the two new widows. She had often feared for Costas's life, but he had survived. It was different for her friends, and she deeply grieved their loss.

The martyrs' story drew worldwide attention, focusing prayer on these lost tribes and drawing many new recruits willing to take up the call. In early October 1968, RBMU sent out an urgent prayer bulletin:

> The US State Department has sent word that memorial services were held on October 3 on the presumed site of the massacre. Mrs. Masters has chosen to remain in West Irian for the time being. . . .
>
> Dale had characterized the people of the Heluk as furtive, crafty, hateful, and resentful of the intrusion of the gospel upon their way of life. It was presumed that Dale and Masters were moving through the valley home of these people of the Heluk when attacked. . . .
>
> Philip Masters was from Mapleton, Iowa. A graduate of Cornell College and Prairie Bible Institute, he first went to West Irian in July 1961, together with his wife Phyllis and their four children: Chrissie (13), Curtis (11), Rebecca (9), and Robert (5).
>
> Stanley Dale was from Australia, and likewise leaves a wife and four children. During his ministry at Ninia, Dale had completed the translation of the book of Mark into the local dialect, and was working on a translation of the book of Acts just before his death. . . .
>
> The RBMU solicits prayer for the bereaved families, and for the infant churches at Ninia and Korupun which may

now face serious threat of annihilation by their enemies. It was [Tertullian] who observed that the blood of the

martyrs is the seed of the church. It is the conviction of their fellow missionaries that these two stalwart soldiers of Christ have not laid down their lives in vain. Our God has sown His seed. We believe that seed, watered with the prayers of the saints, will issue an abundant harvest.

Phil Masters talking on a single sideband radio

Costas's words to supporters were equally sober: "Please pray for the widows and their families, and the work in Ninia and Korupun. The killers have become bolder now, and there is danger of further tragic incidents in nearby stations. . . . May this stirring news draw you closer to the Lord."

He then added three fitting epitaphs from Scripture:

- They "were lovely and pleasant in their lives" (2 Samuel 1:23, KJV).

- "They overcame him by the blood of the Lamb, and by the word of their testimony; and they loved not their lives unto the death" (Revelation 12:11, KJV).

- "Be thou faithful unto death, and I will give thee a crown of life" (Revelation 2:10, KJV).

For Costas, his friends' deaths further motivated him to give his all for the gospel. Their selfless example fueled his burning ambition to see lost tribes delivered from darkness by the power of Jesus Christ. For the rest of Costas's life and ministry, Stanley Dale and Philip Masters would remain a powerful influence. Years later he would create a small memorial to these brave men in his Athens home, where it remains to this day.

A SECOND BLOW

On the last day of December 1968, MAF pilot Menno Voth watched the valley floor rising up to meet him. He knew he was in trouble.

Menno's task that morning was to deliver MAF missionaries Gene and Lois Newman and their four children from the south of the island to the north coast for a week's vacation. Gene was the man who had given Alky the welcome news of Costas's safe passage through the Mamberamo rapids. He was a quiet, unassuming man, a faithful worker, who—with his outgoing wife, Lois—had served MAF's Sentani base since 1961.

An experienced Canadian pilot, Menno had been with MAF in Irian Jaya four months. He was unfamiliar with this mountainous terrain, and low-hanging clouds limited visibility. He thought his chart was, finally, making sense of the valleys and protruding ridges below. *There's the river I've been looking for.* He lowered a wing and eased back on the throttle, turning to follow his prescribed route toward and through a mountain pass. He radioed a quick call to base, informing them he would arrive at destination in fifteen minutes.

Tragically, Menno had misjudged his location on the map, steering into a valley leading to a dead end, not the mountain pass he had expected. Surrounded on three sides by towering mountains, Menno banked the small plane sharply, trying to escape back the way he had come. The right wing clipped a

Nyack College
Eastman Library

tree and was torn off. The craft lurched toward the river below. It landed hard, skidded across a shale bank, and plowed into unmoving trees.

Search planes located the wreckage the next morning. Ground searchers were astonished to find that nine-year-old Paul Newman had survived—alone. He had escaped out the back of the broken plane before the spilled fuel erupted into orange-blue flames. Furthermore, the boy had been taken in and protected by the local witchdoctor, whose name was Kusaho, until rescuers arrived. What made this especially surprising was the location—*the plane had gone down in the Seng Valley, just eight hundred yards from where Stan and Phil had been killed.* The rescue team marveled that this, of all the valleys the plane could have flown into, was the one it had chosen.

Their stomachs churned with fresh grief over newly lost friends. Yet, at the same time they were keenly aware that God was sovereignly at work in these strange circumstances. Perhaps this was the bridge for which they'd been praying, allowing a positive connection with the hostile people of this valley.

Seizing the moment, the searchers returned by helicopter that afternoon with gifts for the people who had protected young Paul—steel axes, knives, and a pig. They also brought with them one of the Wikbun tribesmen whom government authorities had held since the slaying of Stan and Phil. The tribe accepted his release as a statement of goodwill.

Against human odds, peaceful contact had now been made with the inhabitants of this cannibal valley. It would take time, however, to see lasting fruit.

The latter part of 1968 was a devastating season for the RBMU and MAF communities. Besides the losses described above, just before Christmas another MAF pilot, George Raney, was lost while flying in the Philippines. Despite the

Nyack College
Eastman Library

losses and the substantial setbacks to ministry work, Costas remained hopeful. To supporters he wrote, "These are historic events, and we believe that the most glorious pages of this story are yet to be take place."

CHAPTER 10

A JOYFUL REUNION

The RBMU team reeled. Sweat and tears often mingled freely on Costas's face, but the work at Taiyeve progressed. Tree by tree, vine by vine, the dense jungle gave way to the machetes and axes of his workers.

Finally, after four months apart, the Macris family was reunited in mid-December. Six-year-old Johnathan had spent his first semester at boarding school in Sentani, while Alky and the two smaller boys had remained at Karubaga. Filled with excitement, Costas barely slept the last few nights before his family arrived, determined to make everything about their new home just right.

When the floatplane at last touched down and approached the sandy beach, the family was surprised to see placards placed along the shore, inscribed with greetings and expressions of love. Alky will never forget Costas standing on that jungle bank, flashing his handsome smile and holding a bouquet of homegrown flowers for her.

The family reveled. Eyes gleaming with exuberant pride, Costas spent the next few days and weeks introducing Alky and the boys to their new station. Just four months earlier the view from Costas's boat was nothing

Alky and the boys arrive at Taiyeve for the first time

but thick jungle to the water's edge. Now the land was cleared, and the house was nearly complete. It still had no doors, but Costas had installed a working toilet and even a shower, though hot water would come later. Much to their surprise, Costas's vegetables were growing wonderfully; they would eat well. The dream of pioneering this new station was becoming a reality.

At the same time their hearts grew heavy for the small band of new believers at Ninia—brothers and sisters they had shepherded for a year. After Stan's death, his wife and children had returned to Australia, and the Ninia station was left unoccupied, the locals without leadership. Costas would later write,

> Because of the killings, the entire area sank into a mood of desperation and fear. The few believers had to build a single house and move in to live together. While most of the Christians slept in there, a few kept guard outside to warn of an unexpected attack. The month that followed the killings was a long and frightful one. . . .
>
> There are days when the clouds around us seem not only to be black and thick but also impenetrable! Dark days seem at times to give a sense of permanency, as though the sun will never shine again! . . . The few Yali Christians were left suddenly without a missionary, Stan

Dale, in the midst of a wild and malicious community. Terror and cannibal feasting followed the murders in the entire region. Kill! Kill! Kill! was the slogan everywhere. Like wolves approaching their prey, the savages were closing in on the few believers who were left behind.

Costas and Alky would not accept that the work of the gospel might be extinguished in that area. Though busy opening their own new work, they began to ask the Lord if He would have them help at Ninia in some way. The answer came, a growing burden neither one of them could ignore. Costas explained,

> It was in those early days that we felt the Lord's call to give ourselves to the place which was vacant because of Stan's death. The thought of the few believers in Ninia left all by themselves filled us with sorrow and agony, considering the great dangers they faced daily from the hosts of the vicious enemies of the gospel. It was time for heart searching; it was a time that called for faith.

Costas wrote a letter to RBMU's field superintendent, volunteering himself and Alky to serve in Ninia part-time until full-time missionaries could be found. It took months to determine whether this was the best course of action. In March 1969—while Costas and Alky made plans to reengage at Ninia—the work at Taiyeve was prospering. Local tribespeople made regular visits to the new station, and Costas hired some as workers to help with the airstrip. Trust was built. Of three known settlements of Taiyeve people further west—all inaccessible by boat—the nearest one promised to move together and resettle at the station. Select families from the more distant groups promised to build homes and relocate there as well.

Costas, quick to grasp new languages, began to learn the local dialect, slowly reducing its difficult phonetics into writ-

Taiyeve runway nearing completion

ing. With the help of a Dani worker who could communicate with the local people using a trade language, Costas soon became fluent in the local tongue, enabling him to begin preaching on a regular basis. Before long 150 people were attending Sunday morning meetings, and some came on Thursday evenings.

Thick, roving clouds of mosquitoes, thriving in the swamps, swarmed men and beasts day and night, making life miserable for everyone. A small screened house was constructed for the highland workers, allowing them to sleep well. Insecticides were used by the gallon, but a ditch, several hundred yards long, would later prove to be the long-term solution, largely draining the standing swamp water near the station. Still, the plague of insects remained a fact of life at Taiyeve.

Completion of the airstrip in March allowed wheeled aircraft—not just floatplanes—to connect the outpost to the world. Costas wrote of this victory: "The first test landing of a Missionary Aviation plane was successful, and we were so happy to hear so many good comments. It is, the pilot said, the nicest airstrip in Irian Barat" (i.e. West Irian).

The Lord was blessing His work also at many other RBMU stations. The Yalisili people of the Seng Valley sought to make amends for the 1966 killing of two Ninia believers during the same incident in which Stan Dale was first injured. In Kamur Don Richardson reported the first of many baptisms among the Sawi tribe. In Korupun new missionaries Paul and Kathryn Kline saw a fresh hunger for God's Word, nearly one hundred people attending Sunday services. And in Ninia one thousand people had recently gathered to hear Frank Clarke preach the gospel. Many villages previously closed to the good news were now ready to hear.

Costas wrote about the mixed sorrow and fresh hope at RBMU's annual field conference that May:

> A deep sense of loss was evident with the absence of our martyred friends, Phil Masters and Stan Dale. As a mission, we had to consider the urgent needs that their loss created. The stations of Korupun and Ninia were left without missionaries. Imagine our joy as, shortly after the massacre, visas were granted to applicants of our mission for the first time in years! In all, seven missionaries received visas, five of which had already arrived only days before our conference. We had lost six missionaries in recent days and the Lord replaced them all and gave us one extra!
>
> But still our station of Ninia . . . needed workers very urgently, as a new interest had sprung in the area like never before.

Ninia was not the only difficult place to which Costas would soon return. Before long, Costas and his teammates would confront the very warriors who had killed their beloved coworkers.

CHAPTER 11

BACK TO THE SENG

The deadly "cannibal valley" was ever present in the minds of the RBMU team. At the May 1969 field conference—nine months after the killings—Costas and Bruno de Leeuw were asked to explore the idea of building an airstrip in that hostile region. Though initial contact with the Wikbun tribe had been encouraging on the day of Paul Newman's rescue, the climate seemed not yet favorable for further meetings. Rumors circulated that area tribes were target shooting at banana trees in preparation for the day white men dared reenter their valley.

Costas wrote to supporters, "A mistake on our part could add to the already great tragedy, so please pray for us. But what seems impossible today, God can change tomorrow! So as you pray, we will trust God to lead us."

It wasn't until a year later, September 1970, that the decision was made to reenter the valley. Yali believers at Ninia had been praying for the tribes at Wikbun, and one of the Ninia

Costas on the trek toward the Seng Valley

church leaders—an elder named Luliap—had visited the area several times. He'd befriended the tribal elder who'd spared Paul Newman's life, building trust. Luliap assured the missionaries the Wikbun tribes were ready for contact.

Costas joined with Frank Clarke and Don Richardson in planning the risky trip. They decided to clear a new trail between Ninia and the Seng as they went. Costas recruited 120 Dani and Yali workers, dividing them into three groups of forty. Luliap led the group that cleared the final approach into the Seng.

Clearing the trail was backbreaking work—hacking through thick layers of jungle over twenty-five miles. Ten-

Don Richardson, Frank Clarke, and Costas with supplies for the trek

thousand-foot mountain passes towered defiantly between beginning and end. Yet the groups pressed ahead, coming into view of the Wikbun villages on the tenth day.

In spite of Luliap's assurances of a warm reception, they found the first village strangely empty. Had the villagers hid in fear? Or perhaps they were hiding in ambush of trespassing foreigners! The missionaries proceeded to the village center, where suddenly the village chief appeared and raised his hands in greeting. Everyone breathed a sigh of relief. Soon other men came forward, and all began exchanging warm handshakes. Costas and Luliap reassured the villagers in the Ninia dialect, telling them why they'd come and of the new trail they'd carved between their two valleys.

The group resumed their trek toward the spot where Stan and Phil had been killed, now accompanied by the men of the first village. To their delight, women and children poured down from the trails and huts above them, whispering the Yali greeting, "Wah! Wah!" while the men passed by single file. The sound was a sweet symphony to the missionaries' ears.

When they arrived at Silivam, where Paul Newman had been found alive, they asked to see Kusaho, who had sheltered

the boy and spared his life. Up leapt the kindly, weathered elder to greet them. He proudly reenacted his deeds of kindness toward the boy. His actions had ushered in a new day for his people.

Costas and Don talk with Kusaho, the Yali witch doctor

The next morning Kusaho led the Silivam elders in preparing a feast for the visitors. While three pigs and bushels of sweet potatoes steamed in a pit, the missionaries and their crews cleared ground for a teacher's house, a school, and garden plots. The feast that early afternoon cemented ties of friendship. Costas, Frank, and Don stood and addressed the Wikbun tribe, sharing the gospel of the God who loved them. At long last those who'd killed their beloved colleagues were hearing the good news of salvation!

The elated missionaries began their long trek out of the Seng

Costas addresses a group of Yali warriors

Valley, but Luliap remained behind with two teachers, who would soon open the first schools in the region. For Costas, the twenty-five-mile trek back to Ninia was exhausting, but his spirit soared. Finally, he had confirmation that his friends' deaths had not been in vain. As throughout church history, now again the blood of martyrs stained the very soil in which the seed of the gospel would grow, for abundant harvest.

Don Richardson spoke for many in his report:

> What is so important about the Seng Valley, that God should allow so many of His servants to die there under tragic circumstances? Could it be that a submission to Christ on the part of the Seng people will prove to be God's key to still-unresponsive people from the Baliem Valley eastward? . . . If it is true that the eastern Dani and Yali peoples regard the people of the Seng Valley as the originators and guardians of their age-old fetish-based culture, then a submission to Christ on the part of the Seng people could conceivably change the entire

attitude of the eastern Dani and Yali peoples toward the gospel. . . .
To deliver tens of thousands from a prisonlike fetish culture in one of the West Irian's most resistant areas, the King of heaven sought first to win the surrender of some of the main princes of that culture. To this end, He selected two weapons unparalleled for their effectiveness in simultaneously disarming and drawing the hearts of men: the death of His saints and the appealing trust of a helpless child. . . . Perhaps eternity will reveal that no other combination of circumstances could make truth, goodness, and light spring up in the eastern highlands as abundantly as this particular combination of circumstances.

Today, with nearly a half century of hindsight, we can confirm this was the case. The open hearts that Costas, Don, and Frank discovered in the Seng were a small taste of things to come. Two years later RBMU's Bruno de Leeuw and John Wilson, together with Ninia elder Luliap, baptized thirty-five Seng Valley believers, including several men who'd helped kill Stan and Phil. Five years later Kusaho was baptized, along with seventy of his fellow tribesmen. To this day the church in the Seng remains vibrant, grateful for the blood of the Lamb and the witness of His martyred saints.

CHAPTER 12

HIGHLANDS AND LOWLANDS

Costas and Alky turned their attention once again to Ninia. The RBMU family gratefully acknowledged the Macris family's sacrifice, the burden it added to their expanding work in the Lakes Plains. But Ninia needed someone, and the Macrises' previous experience there made them well-suited for the task. Bruno and Marlys deLeeuw were also assigned to Ninia, but a medical emergency forced them to leave soon on early furlough.

So it was that the Macrises began to split their time between the cold mist of the highlands and the sweltering swamps of the lowlands. For a year and a half they alternated monthly between the endangered new believers of Ninia and the pioneering efforts of Taiyeve. Costas would later write honestly about the difficulty of his decision:

It is often thought that missionaries are men of extraordinary courage and fearlessness. This is not true. At least it was not true in our case. I was afraid to volunteer to go to Ninia. My flesh hated the thought of it. I knew Ninia better than most of our living missionaries, and I was fully aware of what such a decision to go there could bring about for me and my family.

Nevertheless, there was no doubt about it. The Lord I loved and served was calling me to volunteer to help in the Ninia work. This was not a courageous decision. It was plainly a decision of obedience and trust. Nevertheless, during those days we did not have the faith to see the great blessings that lay ahead, the triumphs of the gospel, the opening of the surrounding valleys, and the prospects for the Cannibal Valley itself! If I had had the ability to foresee the blessings, we would have had no difficulty volunteering, and we would need no faith to do so. *It is always this way, that blessings from the hand of God are hidden in obedience and trust—not in human courage and strength, but in dependence upon Him!*

Before taking Alky with him, Costas made a quick, two-day trip to Ninia to check on the work and make plans. His heart rejoiced! All the children he'd previously enrolled in school were still there. Many of them were little preachers of the gospel. It was obvious that the persecutions and trials had strengthened the young church. He returned for Alky and the boys—including their newest baby, Alexander—aware that many opportunities and challenges lay ahead.

They first built a house for the family. Costas had just finished building their third house, the one at Taiyeve; this was to be their fourth. "Praise God," Costas wrote, "If He asks me to [build] again, I will, as many as He wants!"

He then began to gather workers for other building projects—many large aluminum-roofed buildings, several secondary aluminum-roofed structures, and many thatched dwellings and service buildings. The airstrip was lengthened, and more motor roads and bridges were constructed between mission stations. Days were filled with hard labor, and evenings giving spiritual guidance to young believers. Costas relearned the local dialect with the help of villagers, and soon he was once again preparing and mimeographing school materials and gospel lessons in this people's language.

The spiritual tide had turned at Ninia. The area which Stan Dale had lamented as so resistant to the gospel was now awakened and thirsty for spiritual truth. The same was happening in valley after valley to the east and west and south. The Macrises could scarcely believe it. God's Spirit was powerfully at work. Places sprinkled with the blood of God's saints began to bloom with hope for better days and the promise of a glorious church. In village after village people would sit daily to listen to God's Word. Whole areas were burning their occult fetishes, and soon four valleys were completely free of them.

Costas began training "witness men" and soon placed eighteen evangelist-teachers throughout a wide region surrounding Ninia. With the help of local believers, these men taught about God's love and salvation. Costas would later write, "It is so glorious to our eyes, it seems like fiction—unbelievable and precious!"

All of this, yes, but the work progressed at Taiyeve as well. Large aluminum-roofed buildings began to rise, the airstrip was extended, a new school building took shape, and drainage ditches were dug for relief from mosquitoes. Huge gardens were tended to feed the highland workers. Costas led canoe explorations into the further reaches of the Lakes Plains—particularly the Rouffer River region—planning to appoint Dani evangelists to these new areas.

One young man, Takenban, a recent graduate from RBMU's Highland Dani Bible School, came to help at Taiyeve. This was a special blessing; with Costas and Alky splitting their time with Ninia, Takenban helped fill the gap, holding meetings with the tribesmen in their language and visiting homes.

As Costas reflected on this season, weariness seemed to drip from his pen:

> Traveling back and forth nearly every month between the coldest and the hottest stations of our mission, straining to minister in two different language areas, facing our greatest construction challenge, launching into expansion in many new points and valleys of Ninia and distant parts of the swampy Lakes Plains, having as many as seventy-five workers (evangelists, teachers, builders, etc.) spread hundreds of miles apart, organizing and planning, ordering supplies to keep the operation going, maintaining equipment, trekking and traveling, agonizing over bills pending and funds lacking to keep the work running, studying languages, setting up schools, writing and printing school materials, caring for the medical needs of an ever-increasing area, etc., etc., place a heavy drain on our energies.

Often exhausted and overwhelmed by the demands, Costas maintained the reputation that he could do the work of four men. He possessed an unusual capacity for hard labor, matched only by the breadth of his strategic vision. Would he have wanted to live any other way? Not at all. He lived daily with Stan's and Phil's example before him.

By November 1971 the deLeeuw family was back in Ninia full-time, and the Macrises once again turned their attention solely to the Lakes Plains. Costas and Alky were honored that God had used them at this strategic point in Ninia's history, yet fully aware that the honor was God's alone.

> As we took off with the small Cessna out of Ninia for the last time [wrote Costas], I looked down and I thought of the days when with trembling heart I had said, "Yes, Lord, here I am. Send me!" God now had replaced that

fear with many blessings! Looking down as we flew over our valleys, I saw the teachers' houses, the school buildings dotting beautifully the many villages in our cloud-abiding mountains. There was Kini, the place they tried to kill Stan the first time. . . . Now a church building was up! There was Yptigeik, where I once had a dangerous encounter, but here, too, what a change! There, in the midst of the village, a large meeting place stood as witness of the power of God.

On and on we flew until the valleys were lost in the clouds which perennially cover these high regions. The valleys stood behind us, but only in a physical way; spiritually, these valleys will always stand before us as witness to God's greatness and power. For us the Ninia story is the demonstration of victory over the impossible. We clearly know now that only as we attempt great things for God can we expect great things from God. So as we go on to new spheres of ministry, to new horizons, we want to trust God for great blessings. Our God is capable of greater miracles and more wonderful things.

CHAPTER 13

FULL-TIME AT TAIYEVE

At first Costas assumed there were no outside influences that would compete with their work in the Lakes Plains. But during each dry season crocodile hunters invaded the region, seeking to make their fortune. Some of these were unscrupulous men, bringing with them all the worst from the outside world. Others were Catholic, likely to spread word that Catholic teachers were needed here. One hunter built an airstrip on the upper Idenburg River and planned to build more throughout the Lakes Plains.

Then came word that a Protestant denomination on the coast, a church established during the Dutch colonial years known as the *Gereja Kristen Indonesia* (GKI, Indonesian Christian Church), was actively planting teachers in nearby villages. Both Catholics and the GKI were known for presenting either worldly ideas or an incomplete gospel. Costas felt increased urgency to reach the people first with the complete, accurately taught Word of God. He wrote to supporters,

> Suddenly it seemed that the "totally closed" area was
> opening up fast. . . . The GKI teachers, too, are mainly
> hunting crocodiles and doing hardly any teaching. As
> the flooding season ends, we know that along with the
> crocodile hunters will enter new adventurous, mon-
> ey-seeking young men, clothed in "teacher pretense
> occupation," until every village in this sparsely popu-
> lated area is occupied. Then there will be no hope for
> these people to ever hear the precious gospel of love and
> power.

He moved quickly to expand beyond Taiyeve, using it as
a base from which to reach farther tribes. The immense distances made this difficult. The nearest community was thirty
miles away; others ranged from fifty to 175 miles by river, easily requiring two or three days' journey each way. Also many
groups lived away from the main rivers and nearer the hills,
making contact difficult at best.

Rivers were the natural highways here. The swampy conditions prohibited much land travel, so Costas spent much

The houseboat used for long river trips

time on the water. He built a houseboat mounted on two large canoes, with an enclosed hut that could sleep eight people. With this—a place to eat and sleep—he scouted the rivers for new tribal contacts. The boat's weight, with heavy fuel drums needed for long trips, often strained the small outboard engine pushing its load against the current.

When, seasonally, the river level at Taiyeve receded, the launch would hit sand bars and submerged logs, damaging the propeller and drive system. On one trip Costas had to swim under the boat to repair the outdrive. He wrote, "With all the crocodiles swimming around, it makes you feel funny. God was with me, and in all these difficulties I did not feel desperate, for I knew that He was close by, tenderly shielding me."

His first major scouting trip was in January 1970. A few days before, he and MAF pilot flew an air survey of the region he hoped to explore. Along the Rouffaer River they were surprised to find a large population, possibly more people than on all the surrounding rivers combined. By comparison, the Van Willington River Basin appeared nearly empty.

Yet eight days later, when Costas and his party traversed the Van Willington by boat, they found a large population whose houses had been hidden from view by the trees. These people were nomads, like those around Taiyeve had been. They lived over one hundred miles from Costas's base, and yet they had heard of him and greeted him warmly. When Costas offered to locate a station in their area, they agreed to help build it. A survey identified only one spot high enough for an airstrip—a place known as Kaij.

Back at Taiyeve, Costas made plans to open the Kaij station. It would require moving large quantities of materials and workers to that remote location. Further, the crocodile hunters had stirred up trouble in the area, recently killing seven people of the next tribe upriver. Costas had been warned not to travel further up the Van Willington, due to the unrest.

> We *urgently* ask for your prayers [he wrote]. Together with God we can once again do great things. The land must be possessed—we need faith and courage.
> The months ahead, we shall be exposing ourselves to a lot of danger; also, these will be difficult days for our family. Alky and the children will be alone on the station and caring for many people. So pray for us!

Beyond the pressing physical needs of the work, there was a constant and growing need for finances. None of Costas's visions could be realized without money, and lots of it. The expansion into surrounding areas required, among other things, a larger, forty-horsepower motor and spare parts for the launch; new single sideband radios for the Kaij station; and a battery and charger. Costas was not afraid to make known the pressing need. He had learned that attempting great things for God would require vast resources and that many of God's people would invest if made aware. Regarding these efforts, he wrote,

> Large sums will be needed to build a missionary residence, an airstrip, air freight charges, trade items for wages, tools, gas, etc. We do not know where these funds will come from, but what we do know is that God wants these people to hear and that they must hear *now*. We feel you should know this need, but you should *not* feel obliged to send anything unless *God* speaks to your heart in a special way. Personally, we do not doubt that He will provide. It is His work, and He does not want that any should perish, but that all shall come to repentance [see 2 Peter 3:9].

Later he would write regarding the life of faith,

> As we push now further and further away [from Taiyeve], we know that we challenge God in a great-

er way. But I do not feel that our God is one who can provide only when our needs are small. . . . He delights Himself with the impossible; He loves to see us trust Him and hang on a limb waiting for His deliverance. My friends, there is tenderness in His rescue. There is love expressed in this type of relationship that is sweet; there is joy unthinkable. I would not change this type of dependence with any guarantee by any organization to provide for our needs.

God was faithful to provide, and He moved in the hearts of many to support Costas's growing vision for the Lakes Plains. Costas was thankful for any gift, large or small. His letters home were always full of thanksgiving for the role supporters played through prayers and gifts. He and Alky were the tip of the spear, fully aware the work was a cooperative effort.

DEVELOPING A STRATEGY

By mid-1971 the station at Kaij was in full bloom. A village school was in session, Highland Bible School graduates were daily teaching the gospel, and the airstrip was complete. Opening this first satellite station helped create a template in Costas's mind—a model by which he could saturate the entire Lakes Plains with the gospel. Multiple times he would replicate a clear strategy:

- Place in every distinct language and people group a witness man, or preferably a Bible school graduate, when available.

- In every village or outstation, place a teacher to teach the national language, preparing the people for a future uniform-language ministry.

- Missionaries should learn a few of the main languages in an area, so as to communicate with all of the nearby people through, at the most, bilingual speakers.

- New outposts with airstrips should be distributed strategically, from which teachers fan out to surrounding populations, aiming to relocate the people to the air-accessible outposts.

An aerial view of mission station Taiyeve, beginning to take shape

- Extensively use wheeled and floatplanes to make surveys, move supplies—including airdropped garden plants where new airstrips will be built—and transport teachers, their families, and the needed numbers of workers.

- Do medical work wherever possible.

- Establish radio communications between all main outposts.

- Construct residences so missionary families can spend long periods at an outpost, preaching, teaching, organizing, and supervising the work.

- Assault the enemy's territory in as many areas at a time as possible, according to God's leading and provision of personnel and materials.

Missionary Paul Kline(l.) and others, busy at the sawmill

The planes and willing MAF pilots were crucial to opening these remote areas. Pilots like Bob Brueker, Peter Holmes, Bob Donald, and John Miller went far beyond normal duty, often flying from 6:00a.m. until dark every day. MAF often struggled to keep up with Costas's demands. From its bases in Sentani and on the south coast, every flight to the Lakes Plains was a major excursion. MAF served many missionary stations across the island, with only so many planes and pilots to go around. Still, MAF and the Lakes Plains missionaries enjoyed camaraderie and mutual appreciation. It's no wonder the Macrises viewed many pilots as extended family. They shared many exciting adventures together, opening the region to the gospel. Pilot Peter Holmes tells one story:

> Costas and two other missionaries from RBMU were at Taiyeve for a conference. Costas was keen for his colleagues to see the area that they had been praying for, so he organized a survey flight across a then-unnamed lake, where Costas knew unreached people lived. . . .
> Costas climbed in the seat behind me in the aircraft with a small parcel he had made up, just in the off chance we spotted someone. . . . We had only flown a little way when we spotted the frame of a house that was being built right on the edge of the lake. As we flew closer, we could see the guy building the house, standing on a makeshift ladder.
> Costas was overjoyed. This apparently was his first sighting of a people he had felt drawn to reach for the gospel. . . . We opened the window, and Costas strained to look out. As we made our final circuit, we dropped the parcel, and to our amazement it floated down and, as if drawn by some magnet, landed right at the base of the ladder that still supported the builder. Costas was so excited he was ready to leap out of the plane himself. We watched the man climb down the ladder and pick up the parcel and begin to open it.

I turned back toward Taiyeve, and Costas could not contain his excitement.

Pilot Don Beiter also writes of experiences flying in and out of Taiyeve:

While the airstrip was being constructed, we would fly workers to a point where the river from Foao met the Idenburg. One memorable flight was when Costas and I flew a young evangelist couple to that point. They would then be paddled up the river to Foao, two or three days. . . . We landed, and as soon as we opened our windows, we were attacked by hordes of mosquitoes. It was late in the afternoon, and the couple was to overnight there and start their trip upriver the next morning. I had never seen so many mosquitoes . . . swarms of them. I was concerned for the young couple. . . . I recall them having a baby as well. However, they took the mosquitoes in stride and stayed. I was once again reminded of how many of the local Christians (many from Dani-land) were ready to "give their all" for the sake of the gospel.

Stations at Tebrako, Lake Holmes, and Foao were opened by mid-1971, each with an airstrip and Dani missionaries and teachers. More sites were scouted, but growth came with logistical challenges. Costas thought the many scattered teachers and other workers needed better supervision. Great distances separated outposts, often an hour or more by plane and many days by water. Costas regularly traveled by boat to each outpost, each trip requiring nine to fourteen days and burning many barrels of fuel, which chartered MAF floatplanes would drop as needed along the way. Both time and expense were becoming concerns.

For greater efficiency Costas researched and bought an engine-driven waterjet—to replace his boat's outboard prop—installed by RBMU's Paul Kline, whose unflappable manner and mechanical skills put him in demand across the island. Costas was ecstatic: no prop to be damaged in shallow water, and much faster transportation. He could now visit all the riverside stations with only four days' travel.

As an added encouragement, Costas was thrilled to learn that Frank and Betty Clarke, who had been stationed in the central highlands, would soon join the work in the Lakes Plains. The demands had only been growing, and Costas needed someone to help shoulder the load. Costas considered Frank the best candidate, especially since Frank had originated the dream for the Lakes Plains years before.

Costas's outreach strategy relied heavily on national Christian workers from the highlands, especially from the Dani tribe. The Dani church had grown and matured at a healthy pace, and many elders and church leaders had been raised up. Dani evangelists had been sent out, preaching the gospel that had so recently changed their culture. Many of these workers knew and loved Costas and Alky because of their work in the highlands, which led them to volunteer for service under Costas's leadership. These young Dani believers had a burden for unreached tribes, including those of the Lakes Plains. Costas commented on the importance of this strategy:

> To reach all these people effectively, we realized that we could not just duplicate the methods we had used in the highlands. We had to adjust and adapt to each local situation and seek to reach them in new ways. The traditional idea that, for each language, one or two missionary couples should be allocated in a station just could not work here. It would take more than a score of families, and would mean allocating a couple to every eighty or one hundred people for most of these small tribes. Everywhere on the field there is a need for more missionaries, and at the rate new recruits have been arriving, it would never be possible to get enough missionaries for

our area. We felt that the job must be done in our day, and this can only be accomplished through the use of national brethren and very modern equipment.

In three short years the Lakes Plains work had become wonderfully successful. Yet Costas believed, by faith, the best was yet to come. Long trips on the river with Frank Clarke, Paul Kline, and others provided plenty of time to dream together about the future. Costas was convinced that the cost of river travel—both in time and dollars—was beginning to limit the expansion he envisioned over the next few years. In his mind the next step was obvious: The Lakes Plains needed its own airplane.

CHAPTER 14

THE BIRTH OF REGIONS WINGS

According to Dictionary.com, a visionary is defined as

- a person of unusually keen foresight;
- a person who sees visions;
- a person who is given to audacious, highly speculative, or impractical ideas or schemes; dreamer.[7]

Doubtless, each of these has been used, at one time or another, to describe this energetic man—Costas Macris. Perhaps none of Costas's large-scale dreams met as much resistance as basing his own plane in the jungle. On the scale of practicality, this seemed a stretch too far. First, did the jungle not already have sufficient air service by MAF, unmatched in its willing and sacrificial pilots and their fleet of well-suited aircraft? Second, since maintenance and safety were nonnegotiable, how could a jungle-based operation maintain the necessary standards? There was the large amount of money needed for such an operation.

There were plenty of valid concerns over Costas's visionary idea, and even some back at RBMU's Philadelphia headquarters were hesitant. For nearly fifteen years, RBMU and MAF had enjoyed a wonderful symbiotic relationship, without which expansion into many parts of Irian Jaya would never have happened. No one in Philadelphia wanted to strain relations with their valued partner, as a competing air service might do.

Costas understood, but in true visionary fashion he weighed the arguments against, and found them wanting. In May 1973, after this vision had burned several years inside his breast, he began to make the vision known:

> The Missionary Aviation Fellowship has been serving us very sacrificially, but as time went by, it became very clear that it will be impossible for MAF to meet our particular needs. First, for about three years we were getting only a fraction of our flight requests. MAF was not able to keep up with the pace of growth in the work. Besides this, it became evident that we need the control of the aircraft, to use it in a different capacity. We need the plane not just to deliver the supplies and personnel and quickly depart, but we need it for itinerary work.
> Our work is totally different from the general work of our mission and all the other missions on the field. Ours is the only ministry specifically called for the reaching of small isolated tribes separated by immense distances of jungle swamps and hills. To reach these tribes, we need a very large number of missionaries from abroad, which, at least thus far, have not been available. Or we need to make maximum use of modern equipment to eliminate the distances and bring the work together from a central point, using mainly national believers for this task. Some of our twelve tribes are as small as one hundred

souls, and that includes babies! If we leave the national workers without supervision and help, the work will not advance, as they still do not have the know-how, training, or experience.

Costas knew he could reach many more tribes, and more effectively, if he had better transportation. Having a plane at his disposal would save both funds and time. He had been quietly negotiating with MAF for two years, seeking agreement on a special program that would meet the Lakes Plains needs. MAF was unable to fulfill this request; the broader needs of their work were great, and they were stretched to the limit.

Costas described the need as he saw it:

I must tell you that, if a Cessna 185 were just to fly over all our outposts without stopping anywhere, beginning from and returning to Taiyeve, it will take over four hours and ten minutes. Then when you realize that all three hundred of our workers that are scattered throughout the area—plus the one hundred men that Frank Clarke has in his adjoining area—are all coming from the Central Highlands (35 to 110 miles away), then you begin to understand what we are facing as far as transportation is concerned. . . .

Because of the inability of MAF in West Irian to serve us adequately, we had to charter a missionary aviation plane from the Papua New Guinea side for ten days last February. Then in April we chartered the MAF floatplane from here for nine days of continuous flying, and now we expect again the amphibian to arrive for another ten days of flying. All this concentrated amphibian and float work is above the regular stream of wheeled flying work that MAF is doing for us.

Presently the whole matter is under consideration at the US Council. If the proposals voted by the field are approved, we will consider this a great victory and blessing, but I want to warn you that it will be a victory of faith only. On the material aspect of things before us looms a great and seemingly impossible mountain. In God we have set our trust to give us that mountain! Now here is where you step in. We need you to pray—not just for funds, not planes, not permits, or the needed pilot—but for *faith*. . . . As God gives the assurance about this need to others in authority over us, we will need determination and much wisdom to see this ministry established. . . .

We live for the day when we will be able to move out of the rivers; when we won't be limited by the time-consuming travel, motor maintenance, etc.; when we will be able to reach all our outposts and spend as much time as needed there; when we will be able to enter many more tribes, to respond to the many calls for help, which keep coming to us from way deep in the bush and the waiting people. The need is so great that I could not even begin to describe it.

When the idea was presented to fellow missionaries at annual field conferences, it was met with nearly unanimous support. After two terms on the field, Costas had earned their trust. They recognized in him a single-minded devotion to the Lord and His work, and this—coupled with the seemingly inexhaustible energy for which he'd become known—meant that Costas's big dreams often came true. They saw fire in his eyes and heard passion in his voice, and thus encouraged him to move forward.

At long last, after much prayer and deliberation among the mission's leadership, Costas received word that his project had been approved by all four RBMU International Councils (Australia, Canada, Britain, and the USA). He had been given authority to proceed with its implementation!

Costas was ecstatic and moved quickly to form a supervisory board. The vision needed some well-placed advocates, and Costas found them in two willing mission executives—

Hank Worthington and Paul Goodman. Hank had served as head pilot for MAF in both West Irian and South America; his expertise in all facets of mission aviation would be of great value moving forward. He then lived near MAF's stateside headquarters in California, as did Goodman, an RBMU council member who had been a pilot in World War II. Both men signed on as founding board members of the new enterprise, which Costas named Regions Wings.

BLESSINGS DOWN UNDER

In fall 1971 Costas and Alky found themselves in Australia, the result of an invitation by the RBMU Australian Council. The Australians had invited them many times before, but the Macrises' work demands had always prevented them from accepting. Finally, after an encouraging push from the annual field conference, they bought tickets and headed to the land down under, little Alex in tow. Costas would later call this the most blessed and fruitful trip of their lives.

The one condition Costas set was that the council keep him busy, and this they did. Within the first thirty days he preached forty-five times! Their first meetings were in Sydney, where they spent ten days. Then on to Melbourne for eight days, over to Adelaide for two days, then back to Melbourne for five more. Their last stop was Brisbane, where they enjoyed six days with a more leisurely schedule, which Costas described:

> That means we only had six meetings and averaged going to bed at just past one in the morning! This was very refreshing. In Melbourne we went to bed between 2:30 and 3:30 every morning. You might not believe it, but I was not keeping them up. People are just hungry for real fellowship. The ground was ready for a great work of God in many hearts. This was evident as several churches, which had not been on speaking terms for

years, joined hands in common meetings, and many fellowshipped in homes of people which had been ... their enemies! A refreshing sense of love just fell among the brethren. When too many people gathered in a home and chairs could not be found, furniture was placed aside and people sat on the rug, singing and praising God.

The churches they visited were primarily Greek evangelical, which meant Costas and Alky were the recipients of some wonderful homeland hospitality. With typical Greek warmth, their schedule was filled, not only with church meetings, but also social gatherings, teas, coffees, late after-meeting suppers, and early morning revivals. Costas described the enthusiasm of their reception: "People whom we had never met before had been praying for us for years. We saw our prayer card framed in very many homes. Oh, what an encouragement that was! We praised and praised God for the great power of His love."

The greatest encouragement, though, was the spiritual fruit God produced. Though Costas did not consider himself a traditional evangelist, he felt the Lord pressing him to give public invitations during most of his meetings. The results were wonderful. All told, fifty people made public professions of faith after he spoke.

> There was one man for whom the believers had been praying ten years [he wrote]. His way was living a miserable existence. Many had given up hope for him. He came through gloriously. There was a young woman who had ruined her life, living in great sin. She broke down and accepted Christ. There was the family in Adelaide, in which only the father and the mother knew the Lord. They were praying for their four children. Three came to Christ during one meeting. The fourth, a daughter, lived in another city five hundred miles away. She drove all night Saturday and arrived Sunday after-

noon to church just in time for the service and to accept the Lord. There was the husband with his heart so hard that no one dared talk to him about the Lord. We saw him come through at the last meeting in Adelaide. We had two people accept the Lord during a farewell party held for us. When the Spirit of God convicts men of sin, they do not care where they are, as long as they can make their peace with God! There are many more such wonderful incidents, but I must stop.

Costas shared in many Bible colleges about the work in Irian—Sydney Bible College at Croydon; Tahlee Bible College, north of Sydney; Adelaide Bible Institute; Melbourne Bible Institute; and Brisbane Bible Institute. He always received a warm response and genuine interest from the students. At least four young couples expressed interest in pursuing missions, and one young man sensed a call to West Irian.

Costas expressed gratitude for the Lord's sweet presence among their Australian brothers and sisters:

The greatest thing we felt was the great stamina He gave us. Humanly speaking, we could not have endured the torturous pace we carried there. Sometimes we were so exhausted that we thought we could not make it through to another day. Come time for each meeting, though, we felt refreshed, rested, and alert. It was an amazing experience. Alexander also was a real nice boy. He was very nice during the meetings and enjoyed everyone's hugs. Only toward the end we felt that too many hugs and kisses were spoiling him. We too were a bit spoiled with all the love we received. . . . So, brethren, beware.

Shortly after their return to Irian, on January 12, 1972, the Macrises hosted the first baptism of local tribespeople at Taiyeve. A number of RBMU missionaries flew in for the occasion, and fifteen men and women from the Ta'ori tribe professed new life in Christ and went under the water. Costas invited Frank Clarke to take part as special guest. Tears flowed as new believers stood and gave witness of the work Christ had done in their hearts.

First ever baptism at Taiyeve, January 1972

By spring 1972 the Macrises were again due for furlough, as the mission required their staff to visit supporters once every four years. Costas asked for and received an eighteen-month extension. He didn't feel he could leave the thriving work:

- Airstrips had been opened at the new Foao and Tebrako stations, which now made ten strips completed in the Lakes Plains.

- Three hundred fifty workers, mainly Danis, were spread throughout a jungle area two hundred miles long by eighty miles wide.

- A team of twenty trained carpenters was busy raising schools, teachers' houses, clinics, and other facilities throughout the region.

- New outposts had been established and ministry begun at places like Papasena, Taiyayi, Upper Idenburg, Kaure, and Kwerba, as well as Burumaso, a semicivilized area just below the Mamberamo River rapids.

- Under the supervision of Frank Clarke and his family, the airstrip at Lake Holmes was opened, a monumental effort that entailed removing a small hill with only hand tools.

- Education efforts were providing opportunity at each outpost for people to learn the Indonesian language. Lessons were mimeographed at Taiyeve, then distributed to each station with stencils, flash cards, review lessons, and language helps.

In August of that year the Macrises welcomed a fresh dose of femininity to their male-dominated family—a precious baby girl, Ifigenia "Ifie" Florence. Costas and Alky were excited to share the news: "It was a very good delivery, and our home has changed ever since, with this young lady coming into our family. Having acquired our quartet first and now . . . the pianist, we feel that the family is . . . complete!"

The Macris family was expanding, as was the work at Taiyeve. The gospel was being proclaimed, and after five years in the Lakes Plains, the work was beginning to bear fruit. This was why they'd worked and prayed and faced dangers and trials. The church of Jesus Christ had taken root in, literally, the uttermost parts of the earth!

CHAPTER 15

THE FURLOUGH
OF '74

In December 1973 the family packed their suitcases for a year-long visit to see family and supporters. Johnathan and Haris were eleven and nine, Neil and Alex were eight and three, and little Ifie was just sixteen months. Another whirlwind tour lay just ahead.

They arrived in the United States just before Christmas and made their base in Wheaton, outside of Chicago. Gracious friends made available both a house and a car free of charge.

Shortly after the New Year Costas began traveling, leaving Alky with what he called the "hard part," staying home and caring for the children. RBMU had arranged an extensive speaking schedule for Costas, with an emphasis on visiting Bible schools and Bible colleges. He was glad for the opportunity to stand before committed young people and challenge them to live wholeheartedly for Christ. This reminded him of his own experience at Millar years before. Just as men of God had spoken into his life, so now he would speak into the lives of others.

Over the next several months Costas traveled thousands of miles by car, bus, train, and plane. During a twelve-day tour of Great Britain he spoke thirty-five times and experienced great blessing. Returning to the States, he did his best to balance time between Wheaton and the road. In total, during the first six months of that year, Costas made several tours throughout the States and Canada, his last trip covering over eleven thousand miles in under six weeks.

Unfortunately, both Costas and little Alex spent time in the hospital—Alex for a hernia operation and Costas for a painful yet benign tumor. Overall the family enjoyed their time in America, though the boys couldn't wait to get back to the fun of playing in the jungle!

Someone asked Costas about raising children on the mission field, imagining difficulty for the little ones. "Are you kidding?" Costas answered, flashing his trademark grin. "Our kids love the freedom at Taiyeve. What young boy wouldn't want to climb trees and have the run of the land?" He was right. The Macris kids were more at home climbing jungle trees than on asphalt streets.

For Costas, every aspect of their furlough was ministry, including time spent with friends and supporters in homes. He was not afraid to call people to task if he felt admonition was in order, yet always with a spirit of humility and gentleness. In a farewell letter he felt compelled to share his observations:

It has been such a unique privilege and joy to meet with many of you and to share all that the Lord did for us in our lives. I have been refreshed as I have seen the majority of you love the Lord more and seek His face as never before. I wish I could say, though, that this is the condition in which you all were found. Some of you, in your very busy lives, it seems, have lost your joy and somehow your contact with the loving Savior. I did share our burden about your condition with a couple of you, but there are some others. We long to see you all walking with, and on fire for, the Lord. These are important days before our Savior returns. We must be ready for His coming!

In July the family headed to Greece for six enjoyable months sharing about the work in Irian. Costas was invited to speak at two youth conferences, a large Bible conference, and to many evangelical churches across the country. He also felt led to start an association of evangelicals to promote Christian music for evangelism.

Once in a high mountain village he took advantage of the slow way of life. He set up a display of jungle artifacts in front of a store, placed his film projector on the car, and at dusk held an open air meeting. Most of the curious villagers came out.

A Greek newspaper article, headlined, "An Athenian missionary among the cannibals"

To Costas and Alky it seemed a new day in Greece. They were impressed by the open political climate; only months earlier a seven-year dictatorship of military generals had ended. The country enjoyed a fresh sense of freedom, and opportunities to share the gospel were more abundant than ever.

Later Costas would reflect on Greece to US supporters:

There are two TV networks in Greece. These cover the whole country. I was on both. The Lord gave wonderful opportunity to present Christ as the only answer. I found it much easier to witness to individuals after appearing on TV, as many recognized me after speaking to them about the Lord. I had meetings from the fanciest hall in Athens to the most backward mountain community. During our stay in Greece, the Lord gave me a burden for our young people. . . . Many people advised us to stay in Greece. We almost stayed. A great burden remains with us for Greece . . . but the burden of the small tribes pulled us back here again. These people are forgotten. No one seems to love them. Now the Lord was opening before us new horizons with the Regions Wings program. We had to come. We are here. We thank the Lord for leading us back.

Of course, Costas talked with North Americans and Greeks about the Regions Wings air service at every opportunity. He was always watching for those who could help move the vision forward. He found one such couple at the Moody Aviation Training Center in Elizabethton, Tennessee. Jesse Loffer, a young graduate of the program, was working there as a pilot-mechanic. His wife, Marilyn, worked as a secretary in the office. They were stirred by Costas's vision for Regions Wings. They and Costas communicated and prayed much and, by his departure for Greece, had agreed that God was leading them to be Regions Wings' first pilot couple.

Costas met other interested pilots, including Cliff Scott and his wife, Lynn, also studying at Moody in Tennessee. They planned to join the mission after their training. These two pilot candidates greatly encouraged Costas. Dedicated, faithful workers were the need of the hour. Hadn't Jesus said to pray the Lord of the Harvest to send forth workers? (See

Matthew 9:38.) These men's level of training and technical skill were exactly what Costas had been hoping for.

Of course, money was needed also, and a lot of it. And indeed some large donations began to come in toward the purchase of a new plane—more than sixteen thousand dollars by December 1974. This was far short of the forty-five thousand dollars needed for purchase, jungle fitting, and shipping fees, but it was a good start.

By the time the Macrises headed back to Taiyeve, enough had been donated to order the plane from the factory. In early February it was delivered, and Jesse Loffer and board member Hank Worthington flew it from Illinois to California. MAF graciously provided space at their facility for the many months Jesse needed to modify the aircraft for jungle use.

The important first pieces of the Regions Wings vision were now in place. But founding an airline in a foreign country requires, not just planes and pilots, but also licenses, permissions, and favor with government authorities. Fortunately, the Lord was handling those as well.

AN OFFICIAL VISIT

Costas had been praying concerning the official paperwork. The island's civil air authority required a special permit, a letter of recommendation from the governor of Irian Jaya—an influential man who had previously commanded all military forces on the island. In March 1975 the Macrises received notice *from that very governor* of his desire to visit Taiyeve. To their knowledge no other mission station had received such an honor. They felt humbled and more than a bit nervous.

The impending visit sent Costas and his hired workers into high gear, building decorative bridges over canals; planting fresh flowers in newly crafted flowerboxes; and, just as his father had done for official state pavilions, constructing a twenty-by-thirty-foot arch, adorned with flowers and a sign that read, in giant Indonesian letters, "Welcome to Taiyeve, Your Honor, the Governor."

When the government floatplane landed gently on the river, it turned and taxied toward the bank, then cut the engine and coasted toward land. Costas stood on the shore wearing his best suit, with Alky in a flowered dress by his side, a red carpet extended to the water's edge. The governor and other officials stepped from plane to float to ground, and Costas and Alky greeted them warmly. After a few words of welcome, they walked to the airstrip, where the governor stood on a small pedestal for a welcoming ceremony. Then they toured the Taiyeve station.

Later, while the group enjoyed a generous lunch, Costas shared his vision for Regions Wings. He talked about the many benefits in store for each tribe they were able to reach, including education for the children and lifesaving medicines. He also explained the spiritual benefits of the gospel to a people who had known only warfare and darkness.

The governor was visibly pleased, and before leaving Taiyeve he offered to write a letter of recommendation for the establishment of Regions Wings. Costas didn't even need to ask!

Later Costas visited the capital city of Jayapura, where he was presented with the highest honor granted by the governor's office, a large plaque inscribed with a special commendation for service to

Costas with the Governor of Irian Jaya

Indonesia. Costas received the award humbly, thanking God for favor with the authorities, for this special provision for Regions Wings. With the governor's letter, the Ministry of Communications provided the needed permit straightaway. Once again the Lord had provided in dramatic fashion.

Regions Wings was closer to takeoff. There was more money to raise, and needed infrastructure to be built at Taiyeve, but no one could deny God was bringing it together, step by step.

CHAPTER 16

AN AIRLINE TAKES FLIGHT

In early October 1976 a small aircraft charted a lonely westward path across the Pacific Ocean, a tiny dot barely visible over silvery, vast expanse. Behind the stick of the single-engine Cessna 185 was Richard Myer Jr., an experienced pilot hired to ferry the plane more than halfway around the world.

With auxiliary fuel tanks both beside and behind his pilot's seat, Myer was barely able to move throughout the journey. The first leg, from California to Hawaii, took nineteen hours. Myer was relieved when he spotted the green, jewel-like islands growing larger on the horizon. He had heard that a similar plane had been blown off course just a week before, taking twenty-two hours to reach Hawaii. With only an hour of fuel left, a similar fate would have left Myer lost at sea.

The next day came another nineteen-hour flight, followed by a fourteen-hour leg to the final destination: Sentani, Irian Barat, Indonesia. The plane landed at 4:30p.m. on October

7, met by an exuberant Costas Macris and Jesse Loffer. The call letters on the plane's side said it all: "PK-RWA—Regions Wings Air."

Jesse and Marilyn Loffer had arrived in Irian months before and were deep in language studies. A temporary Indonesian pilot's license allowed Jesse once again to test the plane he'd retrofitted in California. Costas, meanwhile, busily arranged permits and final paperwork to legalize the airline. Finally, an officer from Jakarta gave final inspection, completing the dream: Regions Wings was an Indonesian airline!

PK-RWA shortly after arriving at Sentani airfield, Irian Barat, Indonesia

Costas with first Region's Wings pilot, Jesse Loffer

Costas wrote,

> Praise the Lord! We are happy. . . . We are excited! We are full of joy! The Lord has done a wonderful thing for us. Hallelujah! The plane finally arrived and is sitting on the lawn of the Sentani airport. We cannot believe our eyes. It is here! . . . Listen, my loving friends. God's Word is sure, and He will bring to pass all that He leads you to do. Trust Him.

The plane's arrival meant not only increased ministry capacity, but increased financial weight as well. Costas now needed funds for a hangar at Taiyeve and a maintenance shop with many spare parts. The plane also needed funds for fuel, insurance, radios, and other equipment. Yet for Costas, the fulfillment of one dream never diminished the need for another. If anything, it spurred him to trust God for even more. Could He not provide for even greater dreams? Costas thought so, especially because they concerned the expansion of God's kingdom. In the same letter rejoicing over the new plane, Costas announced that he was trusting God for a second plane, *which was already on the island.* In fact, Costas, in confident faith, had already signed a contract and made down payment on the additional aircraft.

The Regions Wings board—with Costas as chairman—had already unanimously approved a second plane. Preparing to join the Loffers, the Scotts were nearly finished at Moody and raising support. And another pilot couple, Bill and Bonnie Rush, were also interested. The board realized they would soon need more than one plane for three pilots. Costas spent hours preparing an in-depth study for maximizing the air program's effect, to which the mission gave the green light.

Only four days after this decision, Costas discovered a local plane for just twelve thousand dollars—another Cessna 185, already outfitted with two expensive radios and a fairly new engine. It belonged to a Catholic mission, one of two planes for sale. MAF grabbed one, and the other had already received three offers. Undeterred, Costas made his best pitch, and surprisingly, they agreed. The plane was his. So he appealed to supporters:

> Now, how about the money? Well, don't we still work for the same wonderful Savior? Didn't He supply thus far? Don't we plan to write on the plane the wonderful name of our God—Jehovah Jireh ("the Lord will provide")? Hallelujah. In spite of all the immense bills, I told the mission that, if they let me, I will go ahead personally, so that the mission will not be involved. The field exec-

utive committee agreed unanimously to go ahead and not lose this opportunity. So friends here are loaning me money without interest to start the transaction. The group selling the aircraft had many offers, and we are amazed that they chose to give us the first option.

Already a down payment of $2,000 has been made. God lives. The first answer to this need came from our boy Johnathan. He wrote to me from school and sent me all this year's savings. He had $30. He wrote a note saying, "To help convert the plane from a Catholic to a Protestant one!"

Regions Wings was turning into all for which Costas had longed and hoped. Instead of hiring a weekly MAF plane, as they had done for years, Jesse was now flying RBMU's plane five days out of seven—still not enough to meet the need. The benefit to Taiyeve was enormous. Long river trips were nearly a thing of the past. Outpost visits were efficient as never before.

Then Costas described the Lord's wonderful provision for plane number two:

We were in dire straits: In the red several thousand dollars, we had no money to fly in the cement for the hangar, and we still needed many thousands for equipment to finish the hangar and many other needs. It seemed the most inappropriate time to buy that plane, right? What do you do when the Lord tells you to go ahead when mountains of impossibilities are before you? How did Moses feel when God told him to stretch out his hand over the Red Sea and lead the people across? If the Lord should ask you to do it now, it should easy, since Moses did it first, right? Or is it?

Mountains are mountains, and God described them to be mountains. They are hard to climb, but that's what mountains are for. So when the Lord said to go ahead and buy that plane, I borrowed $2,000 and made the down payment and waited for the Lord to do the rest. Can you imagine what the Lord did? You will say, "Well, He sent us the remaining $9,000." . . . No, He did much more than that. Because we were willing to trust Him, He sent one gift to cover the entire plane and a number of others to pay all the debts and pressing bills, and the hangar got finished! . . . Now everything is proceeding according to schedule. PK-RWB is flying and is such a blessing.

The second plane brought even greater efficiency to the program. Once the first plane developed an oil leak and needed a new propeller. Rather than waiting days for the delivered part, Jesse used the second plane to fly to Sentani for a spare, facilitating quick repair. "Bravo to all of you who made this possible," wrote Costas. "Thank God for this plane."

Grateful, but always looking ahead, Costas and the Regions Wings board began praying about a third aircraft, a Piper Supercub. Smaller than the Cessna 185, this design had two seats and could carry about half the load. What it lost in size, however, it gained in economy and versatility. Again Costas prepared an exhaustive study, weighing the pros and cons. After diligent review the board approved.

Costas was convinced that three planes would satisfy the Lakes Plains need, and he soon made public his newest faith venture:

We felt that we should trust the Lord to help us buy a *brand new* Supercub. This means about $20,000. Then the radios, shipping, modifications for jungle, import charges, permits, spare parts, etc., will more than double the bill. As soon as we committed, we received the first encouragement—a promise of $8,500 from World Vision! We know that the Lord will once again do far above all that we ask or think.

In August the US Mission headquarters informed Costas that the Supercub was ready at the factory. Costas had enough for the down payment, allowing Cliff Scott, now on deputation, to fly the plane from Ohio to his home in Oklahoma, where he would install the radios.

In every letter to supporters Costas appealed for prayer for the fledgling airline. That year MAF, with its vast experience, lost two planes and five people. Costas knew the risks for Regions Wings. "We will be careful," he wrote. "We will maintain our planes as well as possible, we will keep all the rules of jungle flying, we will pray and depend on the Lord, but we know that we have no special exemption. We want to guard against accidents, and the best way is to get a lot of intercessors. Will you join with us?"

Though the Lord kept the Macris family safe in the air over the years, they had a few close calls. One day Costas, Alky, and the kids, over the mountains between Taiyeve and Sentani, suddenly lost engine power, and the propeller stopped! Then, just as suddenly, it started on its own and ran smoothly the rest of the trip. Apparently it was air in the fuel line, but pilot and passengers passed several anxious moments.

MAF pilot John Miller remembers another occasion when he, Costas, and Rose Marshall flew back to base from a supply drop:

We headed for Taiyeve, which was reporting heavy rain. The weather still being reported good in Karubaga, we headed up the Swart River into the mountains, normally a half-hour flight. However, the further we got into the mountains, the more guarded the Karubaga weather reports became. . . . Finally Karubaga reported that they were closing in with clouds. But I was still ten minutes out! . . . I made a sharp 180 degree turn and popped out of the clouds down valley, realizing we were in a potentially desperate situation.

It was late in the afternoon, and the valleys were darkening, so they must have turned on the station generator early. Down through layers of clouds I could glimpse lights! After a few minutes of tight maneuvering, we were safely on the ground. The cockpit was quiet, and Costas said simply, "Thank you, Jesus." God in his sovereignty clearly had more ministry ahead for each of us. There's no other explanation. Praise Him!

Yes, more ministry was ahead for all aboard. For Costas this would mean many more years laboring in God's harvest field.

CHAPTER 17

A MOST BOUNTIFUL AND FRUITFUL YEAR

Airplanes weren't the only exciting news at Taiyeve. In mid-1977 Costas and Alky proudly announced the arrival of their sixth child, a sweet baby girl, Manon. The Macris quiver was now full, and though the older boys spent semesters away at boarding school in Sentani, the family was close and happy. Life was exciting, full of purpose, adventure, and laughter. Costas and Alky made sure the kids felt ownership of the ministry, and everyone was expected to do his or her part. Visitors could not miss the family's camaraderie and joy. Despite his hectic pace, Costas was a warm, nurturing father; the children never felt secondary to the work demands.

The Taiyeve team was making good progress. The Otterbachs, despite some initial health problems, were busy preparing supplies for the many teachers, evangelists, and

One of the many airstrips carved throughout the Lakes Plains region

Members of the team serving at Taiyeve mission station,
L to R: Costas and Alky, Teddy and Helen Tular, Brian Perkins,
Rose Marshall, Keith Barker, Anna and Jurgen Otterbach

medical workers scattered throughout the Lakes Plains and handling administrative tasks for Regions Wings. Rose Marshall, too, was integral—station nurse and coordinator of medical efforts at the many outposts. And the Loffers played important roles—Jesse constantly flying and maintaining airplanes, and Marilyn as base radio operator, particularly main-

*Indonesian officials helped to celebrate the completion
of the airplane hangar at Taiyeve*

taining contact with Jesse during his flights. Many national workers—mostly Danis—served as contract manual labor and longer-term teachers, evangelists, and trained carpenters. These many national brothers and sisters made the extensive Lakes Plains ministry possible.

Over the years many foreign short-term workers came to help. For example, one summer Pete Johnson, a builder from California, erected Taiyeve's airplane hangar. Brian Perkins, a Melbourne Bible Institute graduate, helped with many building projects. And Teddy and Helen Tular, also from Melbourne, played a key role for a season, overseeing the many work crews throughout the jungle. The Macrises' dinner table regularly, joyfully hosted visitors—fellow missionaries, short-term workers, and others passing through. One visitor remembers the Macris family's impact on her own life while visiting Taiyeve:

Costas and his family lived in a very difficult part of Irian Jaya, the lowlands. I was shocked to see the area—a swamp full of mosquitoes, malaria, dengue fever, water diseases, and river flukes that can enter the body and permanently damage your body. . . . The people were also not very friendly at this time . . . due to superstition . . . but Costas came with love and a real desire to reach through the fears of the people and present Jesus Christ. I remember thinking how amazing this man and his family were to serve in such a difficult place. We had visited the beauty of the highlands, and this was a stark contrast.[8]

God was blessing the work of Costas's and Alky's hands. From early 1978, Costas looked back on an extremely successful year. "It has been very busy," he wrote. "I can say the last year has been the busiest year ever, and the most bountiful and fruitful year of my life. God has seen us through many difficulties, and we have witnessed wonderful progress in the Lord's work, both materially and spiritually." He couldn't help rejoicing.

- Taiyeve was now a large compound, humming with activity and personnel.

- Thirty-seven school teachers were stationed throughout the jungle, assisted by twenty-two evangelists, seven trained medical workers, and over one hundred carpenters and unskilled workers.

- Nearly twenty airstrips had been carved out of dense jungle terrain, allowing local tribesmen to build common villages, leaving behind their disruptive nomadic lifestyle.

- Regions Wings was fully operational—two planes now flying, a third on the way, and three pilot families.

- Annual Bible conferences provided workers rejuvenation and spiritual renewal.

- A children's hostel had been recently built at Taiyeve,

Taiyeve station, an oasis of buildings in a sea of jungle

*Costas encouraging a Dani evangelist at one of the
many outposts in the Lakes Plains*

where children from twelve local tribes received a
Christian education in a dorm-style setting.

- And most important, the gospel was bearing fruit
  throughout the jungle—churches planted and new
  believers baptized.

Ten years had passed since Costas's dangerous ride up
the Mamberamo rapids, filled with much for which to praise

God. But the increased blessing brought a massive weight of responsibility. Paying for teachers, evangelists, workers, and the air service required substantial funds, in addition to the ongoing need for new buildings, supplies, and his family's living expenses.

Leadership took a high toll. Many workers looked to Costas for direction, and he worked incessantly, counseling, planning, writing letters, and solving problems. Costas had selflessly extended himself for the gospel, enduring hardship and toil, sleepless nights, and dangerous journeys. Like the apostle Paul, he carried "the daily pressure . . . of concern for all the churches" (2 Corinthians 11:28). Costas couldn't have anticipated the life-altering challenges just ahead. He and his family would soon be sifted by events that, without God's direct intervention, would certainly have left them undone.

CHAPTER 18

AN UNEXPECTED TRANSITION

"COSTAS REQUIRED URGENT MEDICAL ATTENTION STOP DEPARTS IMMEDIATELY TO NORTHERN AUSTRALIA FOR TESTS AND TREATMENT STOP REQUESTS PRAYER ALKY"

This urgent telegram on April 1, 1978, directed a friend of the Macrises to pass along the news to supporters.

Several weeks earlier Costas had noticed more fatigue than usual. Chalking it up to work demands, he tried to ignore his body's message but grew more tired. When he began to lose weight, Alky grew concerned—even more when his stomach became bloated with fluids. On the mission doctor's advice, Costas went to rest and recuperate at a highland station. The cool mountain air refreshed his mind, but his body continued to struggle. The short stay solved nothing, and soon Costas had lost twenty-five pounds, noticeably sicker by the day.

RBMU's medical staff became concerned over his new difficulty breathing and continued weight loss, and the jungle didn't offer the modern facilities he needed. So they urged Costas to seek immediate out-of-country hospitalization, and in a few days he was admitted to a hospital in Cairns, a small city in northern Australia.

Costas lay on his sickbed, far from his beloved family and the consuming work, reflecting on all God had done in the Lakes Plains. Now, between medical tests, blood drawings, and examinations in a lonely hospital room, the weight of his calling settled into his tired bones. Questions loomed large: Would this be a sickness unto death? If not, would he be forced to leave the jungle? Would the diagnosis identify that dreaded enemy, cancer?

Doubts threatened, but faith prevailed. The lonely sickbed became an altar of renewed consecration. "Whatever He wants," Costas wrote to a friend. "We do not yet know, but we look to the Lord with confidence that His will brings glory to Him and brings peace in our hearts."

After ten days the test results were inconclusive, but still caused grave concern. Two failed biopsies had revealed severe liver damage, and the doctors insisted that Costas leave immediately for treatment in the United States. Costas acquiesced, but he must first return to Irian to see to his family's care in his absence, and to attend the annual RBMU field conference.

Desperately sick, Costas was met at Sentani airport by mission teammate David Martin, who drove his friend to a nearby residence until conference began. There Costas was met by Johnathan and Haris, arriving from school, eager to see their dad. David remembers the emotion as father and sons embraced. He excused himself, but Costas asked him to stay. He faced his young teenage sons and said, "Daddy is going to America to get medical help. We don't know the outcome, but I want you to remember one important thing: No matter what happens to Daddy, 'seek first the kingdom of God and His righteousness, and all these things shall be added to you'" (Matthew 6:33, KJV).

When the field conference began a few days later, Costas was in bad shape. Jessie Williamson, a young coworker, remembers her surprise at his appearance: "He looked awful: thin, drawn, and yellow. His skin was like parchment. He lay on a lounge chair all through conference. We had never seen Costas so still and listless before, as he was always a ball of energy." One of the mission doctors remarked to a colleague, "That man's never going to recover." This reflected the thoughts of all.

Costas's health was the first order of business at conference. He shared his uncertain but dire diagnosis and the doctors' orders to go to the States. The whole team rallied. Jessie Williamson willingly moved from Karubaga to Taiyeve to help Alky care for her little ones. The conference knew that Costas wouldn't return any time soon. So they also decided that Graham Cousins, a teammate from the United Kingdom, should accompany Alky and the kids to America after school let out. Graham recalls,

> Costas told me there were many others he could ask to undertake the task. There were Americans and Canadians who could make the trip easily, as they had made it often. I was a rookie, had never been to the States, and that was the reason Costas asked me! He said that I might never be able to go to America, so he would like to use his need and the need of his family to give me an opportunity to visit the United States. He was thinking of me and how he could bless me in his hour of distress. That is one of the kindest things anyone has done for me in such a practical way.

Costas feebly boarded a plane alone for the long journey to St. Louis, Missouri, for treatment at St. Louis University

Hospital. A top-notch research facility, it was located close to Hope Church, which had supported the Macrises since their earliest days in Irian Jaya.

Upon arrival Costas immediately underwent exploratory surgery, which discovered chronic viral hepatitis with severe liver damage, as well as malaria and filarosis, a disease inherent to the tropics. RBMU Executive Director Joseph Conley informed supporters,

> There is no known cure, but it may be possible to arrest deterioration and to secure some degree of recovery through medication, adequate rest, and a radical reduction in the high-intensity pace of ministry to which Costas has been accustomed. Apart from a supernatural intervention of God—which we must not rule out—it seems clear that the Macris family will not be able to return to Irian Jaya.

The doctor could offer Costas only 20 percent chance of recovery. The doctor later admitted that, after viewing the liver biopsy slides, he was sure that Costas would not survive. But he proceeded with treatment, hoping for the best.

When Alky heard the diagnosis and the severity of Costas's condition, she sensed herself sinking into depression. Already physically exhausted from caring for two toddlers, the emotional strain threatened to overwhelm her. She pulled Johnathan out of high school early to do the man's job of packing for the long trip to the States.

To make matters worse, over the next few weeks six of the eight Macris family would become sick. Alex, who'd just gone off to boarding school, developed malaria and battled night sweats and fevers. Ifie and Manon were sick, Manon crying and clingy. And Neil suffered a severe compound leg fracture in a motorbike accident.

Somehow, with help from the RBMU family, Alky tied

things up at Taiyeve and got the family on the plane to Sentani. There Graham Cousins took them into his care, and they departed for a hospital room in faraway St. Louis.

Graham later explained,

> Immigration in LA was not a "together" experience . . . . Neil went through the lane dedicated for the disabled (in his royal wheelchair). Alky and some of the kids went through another lane with Greek passports. Others went through with United States passports. And the dumb Brit went through another. Praise God, this was all prior to the security and scrutiny of these present days.
>
> Miracle of miracles, we made it to St. Louis. There I had some brief personal time with Costas, and I realized that I was facing the one who needed the miracle. Weak, drained, his communication was faint and limited, but he was full of gratitude for what I had done. I was full of gratitude to the *Lord* for what *He* had done.

CHAPTER 19

A NEW DIRECTION

A weight chart hung silently from the side of Costas's bed. It told a tragic tale.

Each day nurses helped Costas up to bathe and recorded his weight. And each day the scale revealed weight loss so consistent that Costas could nearly calculate his remaining days. He'd lost forty pounds and now weighed 134 pounds. Dark circles appeared under his eyes, and long wrinkles cut paths across his cheeks and brow, portending death. Costas's body was beginning to shut down.

Isolated in his room, Costas made occasional calls to Irian Jaya to check on the work. He also called friends and supporters to give updates and ask for prayer. Perhaps the most significant call was to Dr. Donald Miller, pastor of nearby Hope Church. Costas asked if Pastor Miller believed in anointing and praying for the sick, which the New Testament book of James prescribed (5:14–16). If so, would the pastor and some elders come to the hospital and pray for God to heal Costas's failing body?

Later that day Pastor Miller and an elder stood next to Costas's bed, hands on his shoulders, pouring out their hearts in intercession. Fervently they asked God for a miracle—that He might spare the life of their missionary friend. After the final amen they hugged Costas and assured him of their love for him and his family. The elder said to Pastor Miller, "There were more than three of us in that room, weren't there?" Pastor Miller agreed. God's presence had been real to each of them.

The next day Costas looked at the scale while being weighed. His eyes widened in disbelief. For the first time in many weeks he hadn't lost weight—not even an ounce. The following day he'd gained a small amount. From then on the weight chart revealed only gains.

Furthermore, his liver—which had been deteriorating faster than his body could restore it—began to heal. The doctors were amazed, and one remarked, "Mr. Macris, when you arrived, we didn't think you would be leaving through the front door; we thought it would be by the back door." The doctors couldn't explain the turnaround, but Costas could. God had miraculously answered the prayers of two brothers and multitudes of others.

Just two weeks later he emerged from the hospital, under strict orders to refrain from travel or work of any kind. Over the next few months his energy returned ever so gradually. Alky knew he was getting better when she heard complaints about his confinement to bed rest. The energetic Costas she'd always known was beginning to reappear.

A YEAR OF DISCOVERY

Costas, Alky, and the kids were embraced by the warm hospitality only Christ's body can provide. The people of Hope Church claimed the Macrises as their own, scores of faithful joining to meet their needs. Soon the church found a home for the Macrises, cleaned it, and furnished it with everything the family would need for the coming year. The pantry was stocked, pictures hung, and a car provided. The Macrises now had a safe place for mending their many wounds.

Costas wrote to supporters, "What about the future? Where do we go from here? Back to the field? What does God want to do with us? Is this sickness only a way—or perhaps the only way—God could take us out of Irian Jaya? I had said before that I was to leave my remains there. Has the work grown enough to function without us?" The letter continued with a flicker of fresh vision: "Is it possible that the many letters and phone calls I constantly receive from my country [Greece] are a sign that God wants us to minister for Him there? At this point we have no assurance from the Lord as to which is the right way to go. God has not yet spoken."

The family's bodies began to strengthen, and their hearts found encouragement. Hope Church became an oasis of nurture and healing. The kids made lifelong friends, and Costas and Alky enjoyed the change of pace. In God's kindness Costas's terrible sickness had become a manifestation of His gracious, guiding hand.

Back in Irian Jaya the work at Taiyeve pressed forward. Faithful coworkers carried the load, but they couldn't help wondering whether their Greek friends would return. The national evangelists and teachers preached and taught as usual, Rose Marshall continued the medical work, and the Otterbachs and Frank Clarke carried out plans for expansion. Regions Wings, with two planes, the Loffers, and the Rushes, continued its many flights to jungle outposts. A third pilot family—the Scotts—were now studying language in Indonesia. Two new airstrips had been opened during Costas's absence, and the third plane—the Piper Cub—awaited shipping permits in the States.

RBMU had promised to support Costas's work in the Lakes

Plains. The mission made good, sending letters to supporters, informing them of the continuing need for support for the many ministries Costas had pioneered. This was music to the Macrises' ears. If they couldn't return to the jungle, they were assured that the work they'd labored so diligently to begin would continue and grow.

Costas and Alky felt fresh energy as they looked to the future. The Lord seemed to be releasing them from Indonesia. Was He now calling them to a ministry in their homeland? The question would soon be answered.

Costas began a dialogue with Spiros Zodhiatis, the Greek evangelist and longtime president of AMG International (Advancing the Ministries of the Gospel). Based in Chattanooga, Tennessee, AMG ran thriving ministries in Greece and thirty other countries. The two men had known each other many years, and they agreed that a partnership with AMG would facilitate Costas's new ministry. They soon worked out an agreement: Costas would establish a new evangelistic work in Greece—a new missionary organization—under the auspices of AMG. This partnership would bear much fruit over the years.

Week by week, month by month, Costas's body regained strength, and his ministry vision came into focus. By spring 1979 the new direction had been confirmed in their hearts. It was time to resign from RBMU. With sadness, and joyful expectation, Costas wrote to coworkers in Irian Jaya,

> My heart is moved deeply as I sit down to write this letter of farewell to you.
>
> As I have already informed you, we will not be able to return back to the field.
>
> For sixteen years we labored together and we dreamed together, we fought the enemy hand in hand, we loved each other in the Lord. We had our agreements and

disagreements, but we pressed on to fulfill our higher calling.

Our children were born there, and Irian Jaya became their heritage. We loved you and loved the people God gave us to serve. We laughed and cried, we experienced the strength of youth, and the pains and sickness of age.

We trekked on the mountainsides and crisscrossed the rivers. We built and labored, moved by the love of God to fulfill His purposes there.

We studied and studied, we preached and taught, we wrote and mimeographed, we counseled and prayed. . . .

We felt our hearts burn with the compelling love of God to go further . . . to tell others who hadn't heard, who sat in darkness and despair. . . .

Now God has taken us away, but only physically! He has not removed the burden from our hearts for that land or you or this people. Too many of our dreams there became realities. We could never forget it all. . . .

As you go on and press on, putting roots to your fruit, do not forget those to whom God's Word is still unknown. Do not rest until all the unreached have heard. May God richly bless your labors and help you always to impart a clear vision to the hearts of those you win to Christ.

We will miss our family . . . every one of you! . . . But someday we will all stand around His throne with our sheaves, rejoicing in the mighty power of our God and the love that provided the cleansing blood that made all these things possible. Let our parting words be Hallelujah and Praise God!

RBMU Executive Director Joe Conley also wrote a heart-felt letter to the Macris supporters, honoring the family:

There is no adequate way for us to register our thanks to God for what He has done through our friends during their sixteen years with RBMU. Their prodigious labor, their unstinting generosity, and their hilarious and infectious faith have been both an inspiration and an example to us all. They have left an indelible mark for God upon Irian Jaya. Their vision, drive, and leadership will be sorely missed by the RBMU family and by the national church in that land. We salute our friends and give God the glory.

Then, in June 1979, Costas confirmed to long-term supporters his fresh vision and calling, asking them to stand with him during this new season of ministry:

> I will be establishing a national evangelistic society for spreading the gospel throughout Greece and abroad. Our prayer is that the Lord will make us a blessing among our Greek brethren and that we will be able to strengthen the existing churches as we reach out to bring the gospel to the unreached.
>
> Only about one-tenth of 1 percent of the Greek population is Protestant, and there is very little life in the Orthodox Church. That makes Greece one of the neediest mission fields in the world today! There are fewer believers than in any African country, except a few Muslim states—fewer believers than in Central or South America, fewer than in any of the free countries in Asia.
>
> Please stand with us as we launch out by faith in Greece. Stand with us like never before. We have great dreams, great burdens. We cannot trust God for less than what we did in Irian Jaya!

The new puzzle at last had come together. God, in His kind providence, had brought clarity out of confusion, fresh joy out of despair. Hope Church was reticent to see these friends leave, and tears marked the end of a fruitful year together. Yet in July 1979, with grateful hearts, Costas and Alky helped their

The Macris family as they left St. Louis for a new assignment in Greece

children onto a plane once again, closing a year of transition. The adventure of a new life in Greece was now before them.

PART III

A HEART FOR HIS PEOPLE

CHAPTER 20

IN THE STEPS
OF PAUL

Early morning sun cast long shadows over sleepy Athens. An eclectic group of missionary leaders made their way up Mars Hill's slick marble steps. On top they drank in the stunning view. Across a small valley and above them stood the ancient Parthenon, broken but magnificent, its storied columns reflecting the dawning sun. Looking down, they saw in the shadow of the Acropolis the worn cobblestones and red roofs of the Plaka District, punctuated by Roman and Greek monuments and temples. Beyond that modern Athens stretched over the horizon in all directions, its wide boulevards carving straight canyons through a concrete sea.

From the days of Paul to this August morning in 1979, Christians of every persuasion had gathered on this forlorn rock to relive the apostle's defining speech to the first-century Athenians, captured in the New Testament book of Acts.

The group consisted of delegates to the First Athens

Congress on World Missions, a series of meetings sponsored by the prominent missionary strategist Ralph Winter and the US Center for World Missions in Pasadena, California. More than one hundred participants from seventeen countries watched the sun rise over Athens, their hearts and minds stretching to comprehend Paul's missionary strategy and exploits.

The Mars Hill excursion capped an invigorating few days of dialogue. Costas, newly returned to Greece, felt privileged to participate in several conference presentations. He was challenged and encouraged by the forward thinking of the attendees, including some of the day's leading missionary strategists. He resonated with the central theme of the Congress, how to plant churches among more than sixteen thousand unreached people groups around the globe, walled off from existing missionary efforts by cultural or linguistic barriers.

Discussions of mission strategies and global evangelization made his heart beat faster. He longed to see every person on earth hear and understand the claims of Christ. In particular he was increasingly convicted for his own country. Was not Greece in many ways an unreached people group? Strictly speaking, it wasn't, for evangelical churches existed here. Yet Costas grieved that only 0.01 percent—one in ten thousand—of his fellow countrymen claimed a born-again experience.

When Costas and Alky made known their new calling to minister in Greece, people time and again asked the same question: Isn't Greece already a Christian nation? Why the need for missionaries? The evangelization of cannibalistic tribes in Irian Jaya made sense, but why go to a country where nearly every person belongs to a state church?

This is important, especially in light of Greece's long-standing role in the history of Christianity. Greece received the gospel message from the apostle Paul himself, and the New Testament was originally written in the Greek language. Furthermore, nearly half of the New Testament was penned either from or to this ancient land. Why, then, the need for re-evangelization?

Beginning in the fifth century AD, and for the next one thousand years, the Byzantine Empire had been based in Constantinople (modern-day Istanbul), the cradle of the Orthodox faith. It held the cross high until Muslim Ottomans conquered Turkey, Greece, and much of Eastern Europe in the fifteenth century. Modern Greeks are rightly proud of their Christian heritage, and the fact that four centuries of Muslim rule (1453–1821) failed to destroy their identification with the church and its teachings. To this day many Greeks say, "To be Greek is to be Orthodox." More than 85 percent of modern Greeks are members of the Orthodox Church.

To a Westerner, Eastern Orthodoxy can seem distant, even mysterious. The traditions and rituals of ancient Byzantium have remained nearly unchanged for centuries, bound tightly to the teachings and foundational creeds of early church fathers. The liturgy and icons, traditions and pungent incense—all forge ties to a world of long ago, calling worshippers to breathe the same "divine" air as generations past. From its gold- and jewel-encased cathedrals to the mournful chanting of bearded priests, many find in the Orthodox Church a texture and beauty foreign to most modern denominations.

Outsiders often see Orthodoxy as similar to Roman Catholicism, and indeed the two share many points of agreement. However, the great schism of AD 1054—when the two churches officially went separate ways—shows that their differences are more than cosmetic. Orthodox members are taught they belong to the true church, its dogma and practices handed down unchanged through the apostles from Christ. Though a modern Orthodox believer may allow that remnants of Christian truth and practice remain in other traditions, they are taught that salvation is found only through the Orthodox Church.

The Catholic Church in Europe was similar in its views and influence until a movement of protest and reform ignited the continent during the late Middle Ages. One of the movement's earliest leaders was Martin Luther, a sixteenth-century German monk who became convinced the Roman Church had lost its way. His Scripture study persuaded him that many of the church's teachings were, in fact, not aligned with God's Word. He wrote first against the issue of indulgences—tithes paid to lessen punishment in the afterlife.

Bible in hand, he then addressed teachings more foundational to the Catholic system—the Pope's infallibility, the veneration of Mary and the saints, the salvific role of the sacraments, and, most important, the roles of faith and works for salvation.

Luther's Reformation swept through much of Europe, bringing needed clarity to matters of Christian faith and practice. Emphasizing God's Word over traditions, Protestant teaching was eventually summed in five simple phrases, the five "alones" (or *solas* in Latin): by Scripture alone, by faith alone, by grace alone, through Christ alone, and to God's glory alone. Protestants embraced church traditions consistent with God's Word and rejected those that differed. God's Word was considered the final authority over Christian life and over the local church's structure and role.

Luther translated the Bible into contemporary German, allowing common people to read and understand God's Word for themselves. Protestant teaching affirmed the priesthood of every believer; individuals have access to God directly through Christ, not through a professional clergy. The Bible's emphasis on justification by faith became prominent, and the local church—though still highly esteemed—was no longer seen as the arbiter of salvation by way of the sacraments.

Protestant thought, increasingly common in vast areas of Europe, remained foreign to the Greeks. The Orthodox Church, even under Muslim occupation, enjoyed relative autonomy and did much to preserve Greek heritage and culture. Thus when Greece gained independence in the early 1820s, its population felt indebted and increasingly tied to the orthodoxy of its roots.

Not long after Greece's independence, Protestant missionaries arrived to share the gospel. They met largely with derision, ridicule, and sometimes violence. For example, early Presbyterian missionaries—though steadfast amid fierce opposition—were often taken to court and vilified by the state church as heretics who meant harm to the Greek people. But Protestant workers persisted, and over the next century congregations were planted by Presbyterians, Baptists, Evangelical Free, Brethren, Churches of God, and Pentecostals, among others. Still, the work was slow going. By the time the Macris family returned in 1979, after nearly 150 years of Protestant efforts, there were an estimated five to ten thousand born-again Protestant believers in Greece, a small minority among nearly nine million Orthodox countrymen.

For Costas and Alky, the main issue had less to do with church affiliation and everything to do with Christianity's ultimate question: What does it mean to be saved? Many of their Orthodox friends and neighbors were God-fearing people. Yet the Bible challenges religion apart from authentic heart change. Or, as Jesus succinctly and shockingly put it, "You must be born again" (John 3:7; see verses 1–21).

That's why Costas longed for his Greek countrymen to know the same joy and freedom he'd experienced in Christ. It wasn't about being "religious" or conforming to a set of laws to become acceptable to God. Costas believed the Bible's teaching that every person is born separated from God. Each of us has sinned and needs God's free gift of salvation, provided by Jesus' death and resurrection. We receive this gift by a decision of will, accepting Jesus Christ as both personal Lord and Savior. Good works and religious duty have their place, but only as the result of salvation, not the means to it.

This all-important emphasis on a vibrant, personal relationship with God was foreign to many in the state church. Even today only 2 to 3 percent of Greeks attend church with any regularity, and many are openly agnostic or atheists. Orthodoxy, to many Greeks, is primarily part of their cultural and national identity. Costas longed for that to change.

For these reasons and more, it's not easy to be a Protestant Christian in Greece. Laws against proselytism, though rarely enforced, are often used to intimidate and marginalize the non-Orthodox as a minority. Many Greeks apply the term *heretic* to Protestants and cult members alike, even though evangelicals firmly subscribe to the basic creeds of the historic Christian faith.

It was into this adverse spiritual environment that Costas and Alky moved their growing family in summer 1979. Having grown up in Athens, they were all too familiar with the obstacles to reaching their own people with the gospel. Yet God's leading was clear, and Costas was convinced his life had been spared for this purpose.

Their jumbo jet touched down at Athens's Hellenikon Airport, and on a hot July morning the Macrises' missionary journey began its second major chapter. No more cannibalistic men and women trapped in the Stone Age by impenetrable jungles and sharp mountain walls. Their mission field was now a cosmopolitan European landscape, a jungle of concrete and sophistication. If New Guinea tribesman feared and worshiped unseen spirit powers, the modern Athenian felt torn between religious tradition and secular modernity. Yet Costas and Alky remained convinced that the same gospel that clothed and fed and exorcised the Indonesian cannibals, changing their hearts from fear and stone to faith and flesh, could also tame the self-sufficiency of modern man. Thus they committed their remaining years to sharing the gospel with their own people.

CHAPTER 21

THE BIRTH OF A MISSIONARY ORGANIZATION

Gentle waves washed the pebbled beach in steady rhythm, created by a large white ferry just offshore, plying the channel between Costas and the nearby island of Poros. From his chair under a spreading fig tree Costas watched the vessel power by, then turned his attention to the laughing children splashing at the water's edge. He smiled, grateful for so much. It was good to be home in Greece. It was good to be with family.

Years before, Costas's father had purchased a plot of land near the island of Poros, a day's drive south of Athens. He'd built a small house, now shared between Costas and his siblings as a family retreat during hot summer months. Though vacation was rare in the Macris vocabulary, the family's late-July arrival in Greece coincided with the annual exodus that left Athens a ghost town. Costas could work and write letters just as well under his fig tree, allowing the kids to swim and get reacquainted with their cousins. No one complained.

The oldest Macris boys were verging on manhood. Johnathan, Haris, and Neil—sixteen, fifteen, and nearly fourteen—differed noticeably from their Greek peers due to their adventurous upbringing. The jungle had afforded opportunities and challenges unusual for young Greeks. They had seen God answer prayer in most remarkable ways, strengthening their faith with zeal and confidence.

While the family relaxed, their unusual story created opportunities to share the gospel. This vibrant, attractive family—a charismatic father and nurturing mother with four stalwart young men and two precious little girls—naturally drew attention. Few Greek families boasted six children, but most unusual was their talk of God and His central role in their lives. Most Greeks relegated religion to Sundays and holy days, if that. Yet here was a family—even the kids—talking openly and naturally about Jesus.

A Swiss couple they'd met on the ferry came to stay with them at the property. Evenings were filled with singing, sharing, and exciting stories from Irian Jaya around the dinner table. Soon people began stopping by for Costas's daily devotions, one even tape-recording the sessions to play later. The Macrises sought to influence their friends and family with the joy and blessings of following the Lord.

This was an exciting entrance into ministry in Greece. The vacation at Poros confirmed they had something unusual to offer—a unique family story and a rare vibrancy of faith, creating a powerful dynamic for their service through the coming years. They returned home encouraged, eager to begin their new life in Athens.

LAYING A GOOD FOUNDATION

With characteristic energy, Costas spent fall 1979 visiting

Greek pastors and Christian leaders, sharing his vision for a national, Greek-led missionary society. He dreamed of an organization to assist and complement local churches, with a focus on both evangelism within Greece and promotion of world missions. Costas and Alky were well known and deeply loved within the evangelical community and found a warm reception on their return. Most everyone rejoiced in Costas's fresh vision for outreach and welcomed this reputed missionary's efforts in their homeland.

Yet some influential pastors and leaders expressed concern regarding Costas's new ideas. At the time, Greek evangelicals almost never did open-air evangelism. Not everyone liked Costas's talk about proclaiming Christ on Athens's streets. What about the laws against proselytism? many wondered. *Will this boldness help or hurt our cause as a minority? And if Costas takes our young people for his programs, who will be left to grow our churches?*

Costas understood their fears and tried to dispel them. With proper leadership, a new organization could help local churches. By discipling young people in evangelism and missions, he could invest in the future Greek church. He pressed on. He believed it was time for new wineskins for God's new work.

Over several months Costas recruited a board of directors for the new society—men and women of faith and vision. Most worked in business or in the public sector, all distinguished by their walk with Christ and their record of faithful service, all highly committed to their local churches, representing many evangelical denominations in Athens. Together they began drafting a constitution. Costas's experience with Regions Beyond Missionary Union had taught him the importance of well-conceived bylaws; clear rules and regulations from the start would save headaches later. Costas drew also from RBMU's name, dubbing his new work the Hellenic

Costas teaching on Mars Hill in Athens

Missionary Union (HMU).

Even as the framework developed, active ministry began. Young people were recruited to a new music group called Regeneration; the well-known evangelist Hyman Appleman spoke for a three-week series of meetings throughout Greece; and a ministry to university students was established.

Costas founded a monthly evangelistic newspaper, *The Way*, which contained articles on how to know Christ personally and teaching on every facet of Christian life and witness. Costas also began a publishing house to address the deficit of good Christian books in Modern Greek, which soon released several titles. One of the first was a translation of *Joni*, the story of Christian speaker and author Joni Eareckson-Tada. Its first run of three thousand copies quickly sold out, and another five thousand were ordered. The book was so popular that, at Costas's invitation, Joni came to Greece in April 1982 with her then fiancé, Ken. For the occasion Costas rented several local theaters, where many came to watch Joni's popular film, and after each she shared her testimony, inviting moviegoers to follow Christ.

Costas introduces visiting speaker,
Joni Eareckson-Tada, during meetings
in the spring of 1982

Of course, these new ventures needed facilities, and in this the Lord provided generously. Costas's father, Thanos, provided office space for HMU in north-central Athens, located on a quiet street near the city center, its several rooms soon buzzing with activity. And Costas enthused about yet another blessing:

A great encouragement is the official turning over to our mission of a beautiful hall by a businessman. Last week we completed the legal procedures. We paid only $2,800 for this transaction. The Greek IRS gave us full tax exemption! The taxes for the transaction would have been half a million dollars (75 percent of the value of the hall). Now please do not visualize a five-thousand-seat auditorium. The price of land in Athens is unreal. The hall is situated in the heart of downtown and we have been doing an immense amount of renovating.

The hall, which came to be known as Evripidou Hall (from its location on Euripides street in downtown Athens), was part of a government building—two upper floors with large windows offering a magnificent view of the Acropolis. It quickly became a central hub for the mission's activities, used most evenings for evangelistic programs, university student gatherings, and Bible studies for young believers. Local churches were invited to use the space for special events, and the music team rehearsed there.

Costas's dream of a new national missionary agency had

been fully realized in only two short years. Though he and Alky missed their coworkers and ministry in Irian Jaya, they rejoiced at the new work God had opened.

It helped that Costas had six willing volunteers close at hand—his children. From the music group to Bible studies, folding newspapers to cleaning Evripidou Hall, the Macris children became heavily involved—even the smaller ones. For the Macris family, serving God was no nine-to-five job—it was a calling around which their home revolved with laughter, joy, and whole hearts.

Now it was time to see what God would do through this energetic family and a growing band of dedicated workers.

CHAPTER 22

A VOLUNTEER MOVEMENT

Life on a Greek island in the 1960s, far from congested Athens, had been idyllic, revolving around the rhythms of the sea. Yet on Poros a little girl named Marina had struggled bravely to follow Jesus. Her mother had recently come to Christ, but her father was antagonistic toward God. So Marina had learned early what it means to count the cost.[9]

Marina and her mother were often belittled for refusing to follow the state church. Neighbors, who meant well, labeled them heretics and routinely shunned them. During religious assemblies at school, students were instructed to kiss icons of the saints, but Marina refused. Her teachers praised her for character and academic excellence, but they forbade sharing her views, even during religion class.

One day Marina's aunt visited from Athens with Christian literature to encourage Marina and her mom. Curious, Marina sorted through the pamphlets and papers and found a newsletter from a missionary family living in a faraway jungle. She studied a picture closely and was shocked to see a Greek lady named Mrs. Alky, surrounded by fierce-looking, unclothed native women.

This woman must be in danger, Marina thought. *I need to pray that God will keep her safe.*

She placed the picture on her bedside table as a reminder to pray for the lady and her family. Every time she saw her aunt she would ask about this family in the jungle. Another picture of Mrs. Alky, with her children, further burdened Marina to pray for the family's safety.

Years later, at fourteen, Marina moved with her parents to Athens. She completed high school and enrolled in secretarial school, and one evening at church she heard amazing news: The Macris family had moved back to Greece, and Mr. Macris needed volunteers to help with his new ministry. The next day Marina knocked on Costas's door, anxious to meet the man for whom she'd been praying these many years.

Costas was thrilled to hear her story and grateful for her heart for his family. He invited her to volunteer at the office before her evening classes, which she did joyfully. Each day, from morning through afternoon, Marina devoted time to the mission, deeply fulfilled by each completed task, each a new adventure in serving Christ.

Working alongside Costas strengthened her faith. One day Costas asked Marina to deliver time-sensitive invitations to the post office for an important event. There was only one problem: The ministry couldn't pay for the mailing. As Costas and Marina readied the invitations, they bowed their heads and prayed for God's provision. A short time later someone rang the office doorbell. It was a foreign couple sightseeing in Greece. They'd heard of Costas and his ministry, and though they needed to hurry to the airport, they'd taken time to find the office. They introduced themselves, handed Costas a thick envelope, and then hastily excused themselves to catch their flight. Costas smiled at Marina, then opened the packet to find the exact amount needed for the mailing. Again they bowed, this time in thanks.

Marina's commitment to the work continued, bolstered by such obvious answered prayer, and soon Costas hired her as his personal secretary, a position in which she would serve for fifteen years.

By 1981 HMU was a hive of activity, with six full-time workers and as many as 150 volunteers. Costas had a gift for enlisting people for God's work. More than one left Costas's office wondering how he or she had been talked into an upcoming activity. Costas was nothing if not persuasive, aided by boundless energy and natural charisma. Rare was the person who could look him in the eye and refuse a personal request.

In spring the music group Regeneration, gaining maturity and confidence, obtained permission for public meetings in fourteen squares throughout Greece, including Constitution Square in downtown Athens. Perhaps not since the days of the apostle Paul had such widespread witness for Christ been heralded in the streets of Greece. Some meetings drew crowds of several thousand, and though opposition was strong, many showed interest in the gospel.

That summer sixty volunteers brought the gospel to both Greeks and foreigners at several beach resorts, holding thirty outdoor programs over two weeks. More than seven thousand people heard the gospel, and some 250 requested more information. Costas was most excited that Greeks were reaching out to their own people. He knew these experiences would provide the volunteers—many of them young—spiritual capital for the years to come.

Under Costas's bold leadership, the Hellenic Missionary Union was starting to make an impact. The Orthodox Church couldn't help but notice. They sent a representative from their anti-heresy department to investigate this small missionary enterprise. For several weeks a gentleman sat in the HMU office, watching Marina go about her duties—every phone call and letter. Marina shared of her faith in Christ and her love for the Bible. Eventually the man commended her for her vibrant testimony, and the visits stopped. Though they differed greatly in doctrine, he apparently didn't see HMU as an overwhelming threat.

Over time, the state church's stance toward HMU would become more aggressive. But Costas pushed ahead with his bold evangelistic plans. It was time to cover his beloved country with the good news of Jesus.

CHAPTER 23

THE BEGINNING
OF SUMMER
CAMPAIGNS

Two elderly gentlemen exchanged greetings as they took seats at their corner table. It was hot—very hot. But then, what else should one expect of mid-July? Still drowsy from their afternoon siesta, they said little, staring toward the city square, sipping their water and Greek coffee. From this, their usual vantage point, they watched the city slowly wake from the afternoon lull.

A few boys emerged from a side street, kicking a soccer ball back and forth. A young couple walked lazily, hand in hand, from the square's far corner and took seats on a bench surrounding the city's central fountain. The square was otherwise empty. It usually stayed that way until the blazing sun gave way to cooler evening air.

The men had finished their coffee and begun arguing

politics when a large red truck circled the square, catching their notice. It drove as if heavily loaded, large metal platforms tied to its roof. It slowed to a stop, ground into reverse, then backed over the curb and onto the square's massive marble tiles until it stopped parallel with the fountain. Its back doors swung open, and within minutes a team of people—arriving in a caravan of cars—were unloading the truck.

The curious men in the café asked other patrons, had anyone heard of a political rally for that evening? No one knew. Someone went to find the mayor. Another suggested asking the priest. All the while they watched the activity on the square.

The team of sixty—mostly young people—scurried about, each knowing his or her job. The strongest lowered the platforms from the truck's roof and arranged them into a giant rectangle near the square's edge. Carpet-covered plywood was laid in large sections as a stage floor, poles erected at each corner, and a multicolored awning spread high across the stage, one long flap hanging down as a backdrop. Large speakers were stacked to create towers. Workers unpacked an electric piano, guitars, and drums. Others unwound and laid cables between stage and multichannel sound board. Girls passed out stacks of *The Way* to the growing crowd.

By eight the fading sun cast building-shaped shadows over the quickly filling square. A row of lights illuminated the massive orange, red, and green awning. The squeal of an electric guitar cut through the crowd's murmur, and the show was underway.

For two hours the gospel of Jesus Christ was presented through contemporary music and spoken word. Sojourners, a band from Thessaloniki, joined Regeneration and the Disciples, which Johnathan Macris had formed during his first year at Moody Bible Institute in Chicago. The massive speakers carried the music and preaching far into the sur-

Summer evangelistic campaign on a summer night in Greece

rounding neighborhoods. It also drowned out the occasional screamers—angry Orthodox and fanatical anarchists—who tried to disrupt the program. As many as two thousand stood in the square and listened, many hearing the gospel's simple message for the first time.

At about ten a final invitation wound up the event, and most dispersed. But small groups around the square talked, a few arguing, while others prayed. Christians answered questions, proclaimed testimonies, weighed and balanced arguments—the gospel doing its work in people's hearts.

By 1:00a.m. the truck had been reloaded, the last conversations were wrapping up, and heaven was rejoicing over new names written in the Lamb's Book of Life. The caravan wound its way over country roads an hour or two back to their campsite, the gospel warriors tired but full of joy. Most were asleep by three, to be awakened by the morning sun in a few hours. Could anything bring more delight than working in God's harvest field?

They would repeat this routine most days of July 1982, presenting the gospel to thousands of countrymen, distributing tens of thousands of evangelistic newspapers, driving

A unique opportunity to partner with an orthodox priest during an early campaign

An answer to prayer… local believers provide food for the campaign's participants

thousands of kilometers. They preached the good news in many major cities of Greece—even the main squares of Athens and Thessaloniki.

HMU would do the same for the next twenty summers in every corner of the country, exposing hundreds of thousands to the gospel. These summer programs also provided practical experience to evangelical youth, training them in personal evangelism. In fact, many of today's evangelical leaders in Greece credit these campaigns as important in their preparation for ministry.

Another important benefit was the breakdown of walls between groups of believers. As in most countries, Greece has seen disagreements between evangelical denominations over doctrinal issues or Christian practice. Separate denominational summer camps and retreats also made it difficult for young people to mix. Costas invited youth from all evangelical stripes to join summer campaigns. He didn't downplay differences, but he encouraged cooperation to help bridge the divides. Young people who served, traveled, and ate together over a summer developed friendships. In fact, more than a few campaign friendships resulted in marriages

*An historic event: Sharing Christ in Athens's Constitution Square,
at the base of Greece's parliament building*

that united families from different denominations.

Costas was initially criticized for his bold style of evangelism, but once people saw God blessing this strategy, many churches and evangelical groups began their own summer outreaches. He was happy to support their efforts, sharing equipment and personnel.

Costas could not have known that God would use an upcoming event to unite Greece's evangelicals in a way he'd never imagined—an event that would become widely known around the globe.

CHAPTER 24

STORM CLOUDS GATHER

Back in spring 1981 sixteen-year-old Konstantine sat gingerly on the edge of a well-worn couch in Costas's HMU office. He spoke quietly, obviously distressed, about his difficult situation. "My parents divorced when I was young, and my dad married another woman. I've enjoyed meeting with Christian young people that I recently met, but now that's been taken away. I want to obey God, but I'm not sure how. Can you tell me what to do?"

Konstantine had recently come to faith in Christ. His family was from Athens, but he'd been temporarily living in a small town near Corinth while his dad conducted business there. He'd become friends with crew members from the Christian hospital ship *Anastasis* ("Resurrection") while it underwent repairs nearby. The large vessel was being transformed from a cruise ship into a floating medical oasis that would deliver hope and free medical care to the neediest countries of the world. Teams from the ship had distributed medical supplies in his town after a severe earthquake, also sharing the gospel in open-air meetings. Konstantine had watched from a distance, intrigued, until he and his friends engaged in conversation with one of the foreigners.

Uncharacteristically, the young man opened his heart that evening, spilling his sadness over his parents' divorce. He lived with his dad but was sad that his parents would never reconcile. The crew member, named Dick, listened carefully, then prayed for Konstantine and his family. He invited Konstantine to visit the ship when he had a chance. Konstantine promised he would.

A few days later a wide-eyed Konstantine followed Dick from deck to deck aboard the massive ship. Dick provided a thorough tour of the vessel's many interesting compartments. Then they joined the crew for dinner. The ship's staff greeted Konstantine with genuine warmth. He was invited to return, and soon his father was dropping him off on a regular basis.

Konstantine joined in Bible studies and interacted with the crew, and what he learned and saw excited him. Here were families that truly loved each other and had committed themselves to helping the world's less fortunate. Their faith in God was fresh and authentic; they talked as though they knew God personally, and he desired what his new friends possessed.

Then, without warning, Konstantine's world was shaken again. His mother, whom the crew had never met, became aware of her son's involvement with the *Anastasis*. She had heard of religious cults that brainwashed and kidnapped young people off the streets of Athens. Scared for her son, she filed a restraining order to keep him away from the ship. Konstantine was forced to comply.

Upset and confused, the boy met one last time with the ship's chaplain, Alan Williams, who encouraged him to trust God and obey his parents. "We love having you here," Williams said. "But you must obey your mother. The Bible is clear that children are to obey their parents."

Konstantine was heartbroken. How could he move forward in his faith if he couldn't study the Bible with other believers? Alan had an idea. "Konstantine, you can't come to the ship, but I know of a meeting in downtown Athens that you can attend. There are many young people there. It will be a good place for Bible study and fellowship."

Alan looked up an address, then wrote it on a piece of paper:

Costas Macris
Youth Meetings
Monday Evenings
Euripides Street
Athens

He handed it to Konstantine.

As Konstantine walked down the ship's gangway, he looked again at the slip of paper. Monday evening was days away. He decided to look up Mr. Macris' number that afternoon. Perhaps he could visit right away.

And so here he was in HMU's office, pouring out his story. He finished and felt a rush of embarrassment. He glanced at the floor and shifted his weight. It wasn't like him to share his fears and deepest thoughts with a complete stranger.

Costas's heart went out to the boy. As a father with teenage sons, he felt an extra measure of empathy. But because of the boy's age, he must measure his words wisely. Greek anti-proselytism laws were clear regarding manipulation of minors. Costas invited Marina to sit in as a witness. He assured his young visitor that God loved him and had a beautiful plan for his life, even when circumstances seemed otherwise. Delighted that Konstantine had come to Christ, he also encouraged the boy to obey his parents.

"This is one of the Ten Commandments," said Costas, echoing Alan Williams. "In fact, it's the only command that has a promise attached, a promise of long life. Konstantine, no matter how you feel, I encourage you to obey your parents. If that means not going to Christian meetings for now, then you need to obey."

Konstantine was disappointed, but he received the advice graciously. Costas offered encouragement and prayer, and the boy left with a peaceful heart. He gladly accepted a Modern Greek New Testament, determined to continue his new relationship with God.

How this one meeting would alter the course of their lives! A pending storm would threaten to destroy HMU and the work of the *Anastasis*, as well as the gospel's success in Greece.

A SEASON OF TRIALS

Jump ahead to fall 1984. A soft breeze blew gently over the azure waters of Honolulu, Hawaii. The Mercy Ship *Anastasis*, two years on from its retrofit in Greece, rocked gently at anchor in the bay. The crew awaited their next assignment. Since the Mediterranean, the ship had traveled to the United States to rally support and personnel before carrying relief supplies to war-torn Guatemala. It then delivered food and materials to the cyclone-ravaged South Pacific islands, Fiji and Tonga.

Don Stephens, founder and executive director of Mercy Ships, was pleased with the ship's work so far. His gaze was set on charting the ship's expanding future. A phone call, however, abruptly pulled him back to the past—a shore-to-ship call from his Greek friend, Costas Macris. The news was not good.

"Don, you may remember a young boy who accepted the Lord when you were under repair here in Greece," said Costas.

Don searched his memory. When Costas shared some

details about Konstantine, the picture came clear. "Oh, yes," said Don. "I remember now. His father would bring him every week."

"Yes, that was until his mother made him stop. Well, that wasn't the end. She has grown increasingly enraged in the two years since you left. She thinks her son has become overly religious and is now a fanatic." Costas recounted a chain of shocking events. First threatening phone messages were left on HMU's message system and at the Macris home. Then came a violent attack on the office during broad daylight. The front windows were smashed and the front door was damaged with a hammer.

In early 1982 the mother contacted newspapers and TV stations, accusing both Costas and the *Anastasis* crew of brainwashing her son to exploit him and take him out of the country. The media, eager to feed on a grand story, ran front-page headlines like "They are stealing my child from me." Costas and Mercy Ships were accused of kidnapping and keeping children in dungeons before transferring them to slave camps in Switzerland. Television stations picked up the story, and Costas was invited to respond on a national broadcast. He gladly used the opportunity to present the gospel clearly. Yet the accusations had only increased.

Costas continued, "The boy's mother is taking me to court on charges of kidnapping and proselytism. And you and Alan Williams are named as defendants as well!"

Don could scarcely believe what he was hearing. Did anyone truly believe they were stealing children and harming them? It would be easy to disprove these ludicrous charges in a court of law. And proselytism? How could they be accused of trying to change Konstantine's religion? They were Christians who'd preached the gospel in a Christian country. Wasn't this the land where much of the New Testament had been written?

The trial was set for mid-September, but Costas would ask

for an extension. Don and Alan were being tried in absentia, meaning there was no real expectation they would appear in court. The fact that Greek authorities had not contacted them made this clear. Costas, however, enjoyed no such luxury.

Don hung up and exhaled deeply, amazed that a court could take such ridiculous charges seriously. It hardly seemed worth any attention, except that Costas would face the court alone if he and Alan didn't return. The two men talked with their families and searched their hearts. Was this really their battle? It would seriously disrupt Mercy Ships' ministry if they somehow ended up in jail. Was that fair to the crew members?

Don and Alan heard a still, small voice inside and responded with obedience. For the sake of their brother Costas—and for the future of the gospel in Greece—they would return to Athens—a decision that would define the next few years of their lives.[10]

YOU WILL BE MY WITNESSES

On December 21, 1984, the courtroom, designed for thirty, was crammed with more than a hundred Greek believers. Konstantine's mother sat on the witness stand, pointing her accusing finger at the three defendants. "These are the men that ruined my young boy's life. They tried to kidnap him, as they have many other children. There's no doubt they are financed by the CIA. How else could they afford such a large ship? And I've heard they have wild orgies on board." Her voice grew louder. "And my Konstantine—they've ruined him. He used to be interested in girls. He doesn't go to parties or stay out late. All he wants to do is study his Bible and go to meetings with other religious fanatics. Is this any way for a young man to live? I tell you, they've brainwashed my son and have done him harm!"

The defense attorney stood and asked for a mistrial. How

could these men be accused of kidnapping when the boy lived with his father and had never left the country? For that matter, Konstantine was now nineteen. If anyone were to bring charges, shouldn't it be him, not his mother?

The three judges denied the defense's plea. The mother continued, "I wouldn't mind if my son were an atheist. If he wants to believe in God or not, that's his choice. But these people have turned him into some kind of religious zealot. For this they should be held responsible."

Again the defense asked for a mistrial. Again he was rebuffed. The judge allowed the accuser more time on the stand, and finally she was dismissed. The court moved to the second and more serious charge—proselytism.

The Greek government had often used this charge to silence non-Orthodox groups. Though, upon entering the European Union, Greece had signed treaties supposedly guaranteeing religious freedom to its citizens, a law against active proselytism remained on the books. Minority religious groups had been charged and sentenced because of this law. In fact, a number of evangelical leaders had been charged with proselytism just prior to this trial. Costas hoped his case would cause the law to be struck down for good.

Of course, in the government's favor, the concept of proselytism is open to interpretation. The law described proselytism as "any direct or indirect attempt to intrude on the religious beliefs of a person of a different religious persuasion, with the aim of undermining those beliefs, either by any kind of inducement, or promise of an inducement or moral support or material assistance, or by fraudulent means or by taking advantage of his inexperience, trust, need, low intellect, or naiveté." The intentional lack of clarity supported the accusing party in almost every case. How can one who shares his faith have any way of gauging the listener's "inexperience, trust, need, low intellect, or naiveté"? The lack of an objective standard always favored the prosecution. Konstantine's minor status at the time only intensified the charges.

It became apparent the anti-proselytism law would indeed be used to condemn the free flow of the gospel. In this case, however, due to Don's and Alan's involvement, it would play out on a larger stage than ever before. Soon the world would see the remarkable bias of Greece's religious laws.

On the trial's second day Konstantine took the stand, describing his relationship with the defendants. He assured the court that he had visited of his own free will and that no pressure had been placed on him. "I got to know the missionaries and their families so I could improve my English. Then they told me about their faith, and I discovered something that became very important to me." He also described the short meeting with Costas and how he'd been encouraged to obey his parents and stay away from evangelicals because of his mother's fierce opposition.

After several more witnesses the prosecution rested, and the next day the defense was allowed only limited time. On the third evening the three defendants were allowed to speak. Don eloquently defended the *Anastasis* and its worldwide mission. He also gave proof that the ship had been in Greece for the refit. Alan then recounted the scope of his several encounters with Konstantine and the extent of their conversations.

Finally Costas spoke. The politeness the court had shown the first two defendants was now noticeably absent. The judges constantly interrupted his short testimony. Yet Costas would not be denied this opportunity to speak truth to those in power, to stand on behalf of all evangelicals in Greece.

> I am willing to go to jail, if that will help our people win their religious freedom. From early childhood, when I was raised in the most historic Greek Evangelical Church, I have suffered abuse and humiliation because I belonged to a religious minority. As a young person I

Costas giving a defense before the Greek judges

have been spit upon, taken to the police, and even hit. We, the evangelicals of Greece, have been persecuted during our military service, in the schools we attend, in our jobs, and in our homes by our own Greek countrymen. No evidence has been presented to prove that I continued to see Konstantine except the time he briefly came to my office at his own request. And I gave him the New Testament and told him to obey his parents, since this is what the Bible commands him to do. But for our freedom I am willing to go to jail.

Then the lawyers gave their final arguments. At 9:00p.m., after fourteen hours of testimony, the judges left for deliberation. By 9:30p.m. they were back, verdict in hand: "We find the defendants guilty as charged."

The three men were disappointed but not overly surprised after what they'd observed of the judges. But the next statement shocked them to the core: "You are hereby sentenced to three and a half years in prison."

CHAPTER 25

LETTING THE WORLD KNOW

Bright studio lights illuminated the set as Costas was ushered to his seat, the CNN logo filling the backdrop behind him. Several cameras zoomed in on his face. A makeup technician straightened his tie and gave him a once-over. A smartly dressed female anchor smiled and nodded at Costas, then turned her attention to the notes on her desk.

It was April 1985, five months since Costas's sentence had been pronounced.

The producer called out, "On in five . . . three, two, one."

Energetic music filled the silence. The anchor spoke crisply to the nearest camera lens, her words following the teleprompter's crawl.

In Athens, Greece, a recent court ruling sent shockwaves through religious minorities in that country, as three men—one an American citizen, another a citizen

215

of New Zealand, and the third a Greek national—were sentenced to three and a half years in prison on charges of proselytism and giving an underage boy a New Testament.

With us today is Costas Macris, a Greek evangelical missionary, who is one of the men brought to trial and then sentenced to prison. Mr. Macris, thank you for being with us . . .

FOR THE GOOD OF GREECE

After the court had read their shocking decision, the defense attorney had approached the bench and asked to appeal the ruling. The judges seemed to ignore the request and ordered the defendants' passports gathered. Then, without explanation, the passports were returned. The three men were free on appeal, able to travel without restriction until the new court date.

Costas was surprised, but grateful. He'd expected to be locked up immediately; his suitcases were packed in the car.

Talking with members of the press during the appeal process

Prison was still likely, but the men knew this turn of events was in their favor. They wasted no time devising a strategy, including making their situation known around the world.

Don and Alan left for America, and Costas followed a few months later. Mercy Ships was then a part of the well-known mission organization Youth with a Mission, providing the "Athens Three" a large audience. Costas had many friends and admirers after his work in Indonesia. Within weeks multiple widely distributed newsletters and Christian periodicals had published interviews with the men, describing their case.

Then James Dobson, host of America's popular radio program *Focus on the Family,* conducted a two-segment interview with Don. CBN's *700 Club* hosted Costas, and he quickly accepted a request from the secular news network CNN. Even *Time* magazine ran a short article about the trial. Dozens of outlets—large and small, Christian and secular— ran the story.

More was at stake than the men's personal freedom. The trial and its publicity made known Greece's spiritual needs to the world. Most Christians had never considered Greece a land in need of the gospel. Wasn't it already a Christian country? The men hoped worldwide publicity might result in greater freedoms for Greece's evangelicals. Their supporters initiated a letter-writing campaign. Christians around the world wrote to Greek officials expressing their displeasure with the men's conviction and the laws on which it was based. Others signed petitions circulated through local churches, which were delivered to Greek embassies in many countries. By the time of the appeal, nearly a half million Christians and human rights supporters had spoken.

Don, Alan, and Costas consistently asked believers for prayer—the most pressing need—on behalf of Greece, in part through designated days of prayer and fasting. An estimated million people or more prayed for a favorable outcome.

But before the court date arrived, Costas found himself requesting prayer of a different kind—for healing from cancer.

TO FIGHT ANOTHER DAY

After his quick spring media trip in the States Costas took the opportunity to bring his family to North America. From May to August the Macrises traveled coast to coast across Canada and the United States, contacting supporters and holding meetings to tell about the trial. They were always received warmly and with great interest. More media outlets ran interviews and articles about the lack of religious freedom in Greece.

During the trip Costas noticed a large growth near his groin. It continued to grow, and upon their return to Athens he scheduled an exam at St. Luke's Hospital in Thessaloniki, where the growth was removed and examined. It was a carcinoma of a metastatic nature—that is, it was secondary, from another cancer in his body. Extensive tests failed to locate its original source, so doctors suggested that Costas fly immediately to New York's Memorial Sloan Kettering Cancer Clinic for specialized care.

He did, and received a direct, devastating prognosis—six months to live.

On top of the stress of the upcoming trial, this was difficult news. Yet Costas wasn't about to give up. If anything, it strengthened his resolve to press ahead. Hadn't the Lord healed him once before, even on his deathbed? Whatever may come, he decided he would face this with the Lord's help. At a friend's recommendation he traveled to Saskatoon, Saskatchewan, for a second opinion and further treatment.

In his Canadian hospital bed Costas had time to consider the future. If this was his time to die, he wanted to make sure his family would be cared for. He called Johnathan, finishing studies in Chicago, and asked if his son would be willing to return to Greece to finish his mandatory, one-year term in the Greek army. Johnathan would then be free to care for Alky and his siblings should Costas not survive. Johnathan was more than willing.

Costas then considered the work in Greece. He knew if HMU were to continue, it must be larger than just him and his family. A good Greek board was in place, and many faithful Greek volunteers were helping shoulder the work. But few Greeks were able to give themselves to the work full-time, and even fewer Greek churches supported national missionaries. Until that changed, reaching Greece with the gospel would require the assistance of foreign workers. And they would have to be recruited.

To Costas's encouragement, the trial's publicity had caught the attention of young people, many of whom were asking about missions in Greece. Costas, an untiring recruiter, never missed an opportunity to challenge an interested person to join HMU. He believed this was one key reason God had allowed the trial. *Lord*, Costas prayed boldly, *give us five hundred missionaries in the next ten years.* More than ever, he believed this was God's hour for Greece. And missionary workers, he was convinced, were essential.

Costas's plan played out in his mind. New missionaries would need recruitment, support, and guidance. This couldn't be accomplished from Athens—not effectively. No, HMU would need a presence in the United States if it were to capitalize on recent events, channeling workers to Greece.

Scratching out ideas with pen and pad, Costas quickly developed a plan. Of the Macrises' many friends and supporters in the United States, Hope Church in St. Louis felt most like home. The church loved him and his family and had cared for them during their transition from Irian Jaya. Perhaps his friends in Missouri would help start a North American committee. A few phone calls set up his transfer to the St. Louis hospital, from where he could work on the committee. Early November found Costas sitting with ten others around a conference table at Hope Church. Over three days the group ironed out the details for a North American Committee (NACOM) for the Hellenic Missionary Union, comprised of separate boards in Canada and the United States that would help send missionaries to Greece.

The new boards were established by mid-November, when Costas entered the hospital for further treatment. Doctors held little hope of recovery, but his heart was at peace. Alone in his hospital room the night before surgery, he felt over-whelming supernatural joy. *Lord*, he prayed, *if it's Your will that I go to be with You, I'm ready. Whether I stay or go, have Your way in my life.*

The following morning doctors removed his lymph nodes from thigh to lower abdomen. They expected to find that cancer had spread throughout his body, but initial tissue reports came back clear. The doctors were baffled. They tested more samples, again finding no cancer. Hours of testing convinced them of the impossible: *The cancer had disappeared.*

In mid-January, after a slow recovery, Costas returned to Athens. With Alky at his side, he greeted the 150 people gathered to welcome them at the downtown hall. All rejoiced that God had answered prayer and again extended His servant's life.

Costas gained strength and focused again on the upcoming trial. The date had been published.

The Athens Three would appear in court on May 21, 1986.

CHAPTER 26

A FERVENT APPEAL

Costas's heart quickened as he watched the three judges proceed from chambers to their seats behind the bench. The moment he'd anticipated for months had arrived. Six days into the trial at Athens's First Appeals Court, all that remained this Tuesday, May 27, was the verdict.

Behind Costas and his codefendants stood their families with hundreds of supporters, the small courtroom and adjoining courtyard packed beyond capacity, thick with anticipation. The crowd's murmur dissipated, all eyes trained to the front.

The lead judge positioned his microphone close to his mouth, then issued a stern warning: "The court strictly warns all in attendance that no outbursts or reactions of any kind will be tolerated upon the reading of the verdict."

Costas strained, in vain, to recognize in the man's expression any sign of the decision. In fact, the judges had remained stoic through three days of testimony. Then the verdict.

"It is the finding of this court that the defendants are—"

TRUTH ON TRIAL

The previous Wednesday, May 21, the defendants had arrived at the courthouse midmorning, expecting the trial to begin immediately. But a bomb threat had cleared the building, so they waited outside. Costas and his friends were unnerved to see prisoners led from the courthouse jail in handcuffs. Would this be their fate by day's end?

The trial began about 5:00p.m. Unlike their first trial, this one had drawn many foreigners, including reporters from Associated Press, Reuters, *Time*, and many European newspapers. Present also were dignitaries from the American Embassy and various European human rights organizations. The first court's decision had been heard around the world.

First on the stand was young Konstantine's mother, the one pressing charges. For several hours she repeated her previous claims against Costas, Don, and Alan. With characteristic fervor she accused the men of attempting to lure her son and other young people by promising them an easy life and trips abroad. She finished late in the evening, and the court adjourned.

The next morning Konstantine took the stand. Again he spoke favorably of the defendants, speaking honestly while also diligent to honor his mother. Costas was impressed with the young man, clearly growing in his relationship with the Lord.

The day ended with a Greek parliament member's testimony on the defendants' behalf. A respected politician and daughter of a former prime minister, she had looked closely at the law and implored the court to overturn the charges.

She had studied several years outside Greece and had enjoyed her experience in Protestant churches abroad. "This law of anti-proselytism is only in Greece," she said. "No other Western nation has it. It's embarrassing to us, and we must change it. If you bring down a guilty sentence to these men because of this law, it will be a shameful day for Greece."

The third day was given entirely to the defense. Several leading attorneys were called to testify, including one for Youth with a Mission. Also Dr. Demosthenes Katsarkas—a medical doctor and vice president of the Greek Evangelical Alliance—and the Reverend Nicholas Tsianaklides—pastor of the First Greek Evangelical Church of Athens, where Costas was a member—both affirmed Costas's integrity and character.

Then came a leading scholar, Dr. John Warwick Montgomery, former director of studies at the International Human Rights Institute in Strasbourg, France. He had written over one hundred books and papers on international law and religious freedom and here presented a solid legal brief for the defense. His familiarity with the Greek constitution and Greece's international obligations as member of the European Union made him an expert witness.

At day's end the three defendants were allowed to give brief statements. Costas knew his attorneys' advice, insisting that he talk only about the current case and not about religious freedom in Greece. But he refused to follow it. Jail or not, he could not let the moment pass without doing all he could to help overturn these unjust laws. Costas passionately challenged the constitutionality of the proselytism laws: "For years I served in the world's largest Muslim country, Indonesia, and I received recognition for my work as a Christian missionary. Now I've come back to my own country, the mother of democracy and freedom of speech, and I am prosecuted for sharing my faith on the very streets of Athens where the apostle Paul preached two thousand years ago."

He told the court that God was bringing the case to the world's attention, so these laws might be changed. Several times the lead judge reprimanded him for talking about "irrelevancies" instead of the charges at hand. But Costas persisted, speaking forcefully about the need for legal reform, preferring to address religious freedom rather than his own defense.

Finally the lead judge adjourned the court until the following Tuesday afternoon. *Tuesday*, thought the men. *We have to wait another four days to hear the verdict.*

The long weekend crawled by. The defendants and their families tried to stay busy, but the trial consumed them. Were these the last few days with their loved ones before prison? Suspense overwhelmed them.

After what seemed an eternity, the day of decision arrived. Costas stood in the courtyard before entering the courthouse and told several friends, "Today's final events are but a small battle in the war to which we have committed ourselves until this land, where freedom was born, can allow us to enjoy our innate human rights to religious freedom."

Costas, on the morning of the appeal, in front of the "jail-car" that would take him to prison if convicted

Again the courtroom was packed beyond capacity, people barely able to move. More than forty evangelical pastors and Christian workers from around Greece, among hundreds of church members and supporters, had come to show support. Truly, the trial had galvanized a spirit of unity among Greek believers like never before.

The crowd spilled out of the courtroom, down the hallway,

and into the courtyard. No one could doubt this decision's significance. More than the freedom of three men was at stake; this verdict would affect the evangelical community's freedom to share the gospel.

Several sharp whacks from the judge's gavel gave notice the court was now in session. First up, the attorneys for the prosecution.

Costas braced himself as the prosecuting attorney rose to speak. Similar in status to a US district attorney, the man had previously and sharply articulated reasons why the defendants were guilty as charged. But now his opening words startled the room. With Konstantine back on the stand, he looked the young man in the eye, then, gesturing toward the defendants, queried, "Did these people ask you to engage in drugs?"

"No," Konstantine replied.

"Did they get you involved with sex and pornography?"

"No."

"How about violence?"

"No."

"Did they ask you to obey the laws of your country?"

"Yes, they did."

"Did they ask you to obey and honor your parents?"

"Yes."

The prosecutor halted for a moment, then turned to the three defendants and said with a smirk, "Can you please have a talk with my son?"

The courtroom erupted in laughter. Then the lawyer faced the judges and closed: "I recommend to the court that these men be found innocent!"

Costas glanced at his codefendants and then at the crowd behind him, noting surprise and dawning glimmers of hope. Was this the first sign of God's answer?

The first prosecutor sat, and the second approached the bench, visibly flustered. He insisted that only a guilty verdict was reasonable.

Then the three Greek attorneys for the defense presented their final arguments, referring to the hundreds of documents they'd submitted throughout the trial in support of the defendants. The personal attorneys for Don Stephens and Alan Williams then clearly, again, presented the gospel before the court, one of them exclaiming, "The only reason these men are being judged is because they obeyed the gospel of Christ . . . . It is unbelievable that part of the accusation is that they gave away a New Testament in Greek."

Finally the judges left to deliberate. They returned at 11:30p.m., after nearly three hours, verdict in hand.

Costas and his friends listened intently. The presiding judge began to read in Greek. First he described events leading to the charges, then clarified the issue of proselytism. Halfway through, Costas leaned over to Don—who couldn't understand the language—and whispered, "We're innocent!"

A minute or two later Costas's prediction was confirmed: "It is the finding of this court that the defendants are innocent of all charges."

Costas, Don, and Alan sat in stunned silence. At the least they'd expected to spend a short time in jail. Could it be true? Was this long ordeal finally over? They scarcely believed they'd heard correctly.

The crowd could barely contain itself. But, under strict warnings to remain quiet, they waited until the judges left the bench before erupting with joy. Wives and children pressing around, the Athens Three felt overcome with equal parts surprise, joy, and gratitude. Greek brothers and sisters in Christ hugged each other, reveling in God's mercy and His answers to prayer.

Costas walked away from the courthouse, his excited children hugging as if they'd never let go. A TV reporter forced a microphone to his face. "Mr. Macris, now that you've been found innocent of all charges, what do you have to say?"

Without pause Costas replied, "Now I want five hundred missionaries for my country to go to every town, every village, with this message of the gospel."

The "Athens 3" with others. L to R: Don Stephens, Alan Williams, Konstantine, Lawyer George Patsaouras, Costas Macris.

Storms had threatened, but the Lord had protected. God had mercifully vanquished both cancer and threat of jail in response to prayer.

Costas immediately redoubled his ministry efforts. It was time to move forward with even greater faith. The doors for the gospel in Greece had opened wider than ever before.[11]

CHAPTER 27

A MORNING STAR ON THE HORIZON

Ken Overman knew boats. And he wasn't sure about the one beneath his feet.

The weather-beaten schooner had seen better days. She was well-built but worn, rust seeping like tears from her glass portholes. Ken walked the boat's sixty-three-foot deck, cockpit to bowsprit, noting every detail. He paid special attention to the two tall masts, his eyes following their metal frames upward fifty feet above. *Is this old gal sturdy enough for a transatlantic voyage?* He had his doubts.

As he hunched his tall frame down the stairs leading below deck, the sour smell of bilge assaulted his nostrils. He scowled and plunged forward into the darkened main compartment. It was simple and sparse, definitely not built for comfort, a far cry from the yachts Ken had captained in the Mediterranean.

Still, the boat had a sturdiness about her. Ken examined the quarters, then knelt and lifted some floorboards in the main cabin. He reached down past the engine to examine the boat's hull, his fingers tracing thick steel and professional welds. *She's solid. Someone built her to last.*

He stood and examined the compartment again, wheels of imagination turning. *If the living space could be opened up . . . perhaps some foldout bunks could line the sides.* His eyes darted. *Could a large dining table fit near the kitchen?* He grinned, surprised at how the boat was growing on him. It would take a lot of work—he could almost smell the sawdust and marine paint, a job list forming in his head—but something told him he was on the right track.

His brain full of calculations, Ken went topside then walked down the gangplank to the dock. He turned and gave the tired vessel a long look. Near the bow faded black letters spelled the boat's name: *Morning Star.*

Ken smiled. It was fitting.

Costas was waiting for his call, and Ken knew his Greek friend would be thrilled with his report.

"She's perfect," Ken said, back at his hotel. "Costas, the *Morning Star* is perfect for reaching the islands of Greece."

GOD'S CHOSEN VESSEL

For several years Costas's burden had grown for the Greek islands. Summer campaigns were gradually reaching every major city on the mainland. But the same method wasn't feasible for the islands. Traveling to and between them by ferry was cost prohibitive. Greek shipping magnates owned the largest commercial fleet in the world. Yet, mused Costas, not even one small boat was serving the Greek islands with the gospel.

Such a vessel would have to be large enough for onboard meetings, but small enough to enter typical island harbors. It would need character, something to draw positive attention, especially from its sailing community. Costas made this a matter of prayer. He'd seen God provide airplanes for the jungle. Why not a boat for the islands?

When Don Stephens, Costas's onetime codefendant, called and asked about any interest in a boat for the ministry, Costas was overjoyed. Don had recommended Costas to the leaders of Global Youth Evangelism, a California-based ministry with a schooner it no longer needed. They'd used it for missionary tours in the South Pacific and Latin America. Instead of selling the boat, they generously offered to lease it to the Hellenic Missionary Union, as long as it would be used for the Lord's work. The terms? *One dollar per year.*

Costas was ready to sign, but first someone must inspect the boat. He remembered meeting Ken and Barb Overman, a ministry-minded couple who'd lived in Athens after US military duty in Europe. The Lord had dramatically saved them from an empty, wandering lifestyle. Now their hearts beat for the Greek people. Furthermore, Ken was an expert yachtsman who grew up sailing the California coast. In Greece he had yachted tourists between islands. At Costas's request, Ken, then living in Annapolis, Maryland, agreed to examine the schooner in California and, if it checked out, to captain it to Greece. He'd been yearning for an adventure.

"Also, Ken," said Costas in his sweetest recruiting voice, "we are praying for a captain who will skipper the boat here in Greece. We'd love for you and Barb to come and join our ministry."

The Overmans had dreamed of returning to Greece as full-time missionaries, so he was tempted. He told Costas he'd pray about it.

The lease was signed a few weeks later, and a team was recruited for the transatlantic crossing. Barb and the Overman's ten-year-old daughter, Lisa, eagerly signed on, as well as a couple of *Morning Star*'s former crew members. Then the Overmans snagged several young single friends from Annapolis, and finally a happy-go-lucky South African yachtsman named John.

Ken was happy. What some lacked in experience, they made up in enthusiasm. Most important, everyone was coming for the right purpose, to help bring the gospel to Greece.

In late June 1986 the *Morning Star* motored away from San Diego's Coronado Marina and out to open sea. They headed south, heavy with food, clothing, medicine, and Christian literature for delivery to churches in Nicaragua. From there they sailed east through the Panama Canal, then to Panama City, Florida, where someone donated money to replace the worn sails. In late summer the boat arrived safely in Annapolis for refitting and repairs.

That's when the real work began. Ken and Barb started raising money and prayer, traveling to any church that would let them share. The crew cleaned and painted while skilled craftsmen, most donating their time, completed larger projects. The vessel's metal structure was altered to provide more meeting space below. A woodworker named Stan Long—father of HMU missionary Michael Long—donated months, expertly creating a world-class interior.

By the following June the schooner was ready. Friends and church family waved goodbye and promised to pray as Ken guided the *Morning Star* into the Chesapeake Bay toward the Atlantic. Thousands of miles of empty ocean lay ahead, and perils that would test the crew's mettle.

ANNAPOLIS TO POROS

Eight weeks later, Costas, Alky, and their children stood with several HMU staff on the promenade that ribboned around Poros island's main town. A constant salty breeze made the hot afternoon bearable. The group's dancing eyes strained to locate the *Morning Star* docked among dozens of watercraft tied against the seawall. Soon they spotted two masts towering above ornate yachts, bobbing against their moorings. "There she is," cried one of the kids, initiating a footrace that led to the *Morning Star*'s side. Ken's sun-weathered smile welcomed them aboard. Costas couldn't believe the *Morning Star*'s transformation since San Diego. He breathed a prayer of gratitude and hugged each of the crew in turn.

That evening the celebration continued at a local taverna around tables pushed together and filled with food. A yellow moon rose over laughter and stories from the open sea. Ken and the crew held their friends spellbound, as they recounted their adventures over the previous few weeks.

The trip had been difficult right from the start. Soon after they entered the Atlantic, high winds and lightning warned of an impending squall. They quickly lowered the sails, rain beginning to pelt the deck, waves rising around them.

For three days they endured tumultuous seas, many of the crew seasick in their bunks. Even Ken had to lay low, his stomach churning as the storm tossed the boat mercilessly. On the fourth day the weather, and stomachs, calmed. A day later they arrived, grateful, in Bermuda.

A few days of solid food and good sleep readied the crew to sail again. Ken steered the vessel out of harbor and pointed the bowsprit east. Greece lay 5,500 miles beyond the horizon. For three weeks the *Morning Star* cut through waves of every size, following the thirty-seventh parallel toward Europe. Ken's estimate of the boat's sturdy design held true. Not the fastest boat he'd skippered, she handled the roughest seas. He was thankful for the skilled craftsmen who'd bolstered her for the voyage.

A speck on endless waters, the *Morning Star* faced some tense moments. Once Ken saw fierce weather approaching and ordered sails lowered. The mainsail became stuck; the top cable had jumped out of its pulley. The crew yanked and pulled, but the cable wouldn't budge. Ken strapped himself to a board tethered by cables—a bosun's chair—and climbed the mast. Winds whipped the fully extended mainsail, causing the *Morning Star* to pitch beneath him. Ken, high above the deck, felt its every motion amplified. He pulled the jammed cable, to no avail. Below, the crew's rain-drenched faces stared up, eyes wide with fear. Ken's makeshift chair swung as on a carnival ride, sometimes out over water. He struggled to stay upright.

Ken grabbed the cable again. Using his full weight, he yanked as hard as he could. The cable jumped into its track, and the mainsail dropped. But the line's sudden slack surprised him, and he lost his balance. Tumbling backward, he grabbed a wire and managed to pull himself upright. Only then did he notice blood smearing the mast. The frayed wire had cut a deep gash between his thumb and forefinger.

Sails finally secured, Ken lowered himself to the deck and went below to tend his wound. Fortunately, the tendon wasn't severed, and from then on Ken sported a nasty scar and an exciting story of God's kind protection.

Seasickness continued to plague the crew, some more than others. Eleven-year-old Lisa became so weak that Ken and Barb feared for her life. But after many days and much prayer her strength returned, along with her bright-eyed enthusiasm for this adventure of a lifetime.

The ecstatic crew finally watched the lush green of the Azores Islands rise out of the salty mist. Since their departure from the Bahamas weeks before, they'd seen no other ships at sea—not even lights. Now, with 2,400 miles of sea behind them, they were eager for a few days' rest in civilization before continuing east.

The remaining thousand miles to Gibraltar went more smoothly but not without incident. An engine breakdown caused some difficulty, and a rogue wave threw Barb against the corner of a bunk, bruising her ribs. The crew was glad to enter the Mediterranean in early August, done with the Atlantic currents.

Currents were shifting inside Ken as well. He and Barb had left Annapolis planning to stay in Greece, skipper the *Morning Star,* and lead the island ministry. But by the time they reached the Mediterranean, he knew they were to return to the States for further schooling. In God's providence a young Australian couple, Theo and Sandra Goutzios, had just applied with the mission, a perfect fit for the *Morning Star* and its ministry for years to come.

Ken phoned Costas upon reaching Gibraltar, and they agreed that Theo should fly to join them for the final leg to Greece. This way Theo—an experienced sailor—could get acquainted with the *Morning Star* under Ken's direction. The *Morning Star* welcomed the Australian skipper aboard in Spain, and a week later they passed between the steep walls of the Corinth Canal. One more day, and they approached their destination, the island of Poros.[12]

Costas sat at the table's head, listening to Ken's amazing stories. He smiled. *Can there be anything more beautiful, more fulfilling, than serving the Lord wholeheartedly? There's no way the world's pleasures can compare to this.*

The Morning Star *in Greek waters*

He glanced at those around the table. His precious Alky and their children were on his right. On his left sat Ken and the crew who'd risked so much to deliver the *Morning Star*. Also at the table were several young missionaries who'd recently joined HMU.

He was tempted to share another dream growing in his heart, but he refrained lest he be taken as ungrateful for God's provision of the *Morning Star*. Now the boat needed a home, a seaside property for a base of operations.

But that could wait for another day. Costas took a bite of food and rejoined the conversation, his contagious laughter soon energizing the throng.

CHAPTER 28

A PLACE IN THE WILDERNESS

On a hot July morning in 1989 a small crew rested from their labor on a brush-covered hillside rising steeply from a deep blue bay. They pulled off work gloves, wiped sweat from their brows, and thirstily downed cold water from paper cups. Clearing land by hand on uneven terrain was hard work, working around boulders, thorns, and wild olive trees. The day would only grow hotter.

Costas sat on a flat rock and gazed out over the beautiful bay. Light danced on the water, a million sparklers racing to meet the sun's midmorning rise. In the distance, near the bay's mouth, sat a small island, a dry brown hump of sage and dirt shaped like a map of Cyprus—its plainness accentuating the blue around it. Farther still, obscured by mist, Costas could see high mountain domes jutting powerfully from the long Greek island of Euboia.

How kind of the Lord to provide such a beautiful place,

thought Costas.

A voice interrupted his thoughts, a twenty-something HMU missionary anxious to learn about the life of faith. "Costas, what do you believe this land will look like in the future? What do you see?"

Costas grinned. It was the kind of question he loved. He turned to the shoreline far below. "I see a large dock at water's edge, large enough to accommodate many people and lots of equipment." He gestured toward the *Morning Star*, tied off-shore to underwater cement moorings. "Of course, as a base of operations for the sailing ministry we'll need a house for the captain and storage sheds and an office . . . perhaps a dry dock someday." Costas's eyes shifted to the shelf of land just above the rocky beach. "Over there I see a soccer field, and next to that tennis and basketball courts, maybe even room for a swimming pool."

Gazing farther inland, he said, "Along the far ridge I see a workshop and a line of cabins. And right here below us a large hotel and conference center." His enthusiasm grew. "And the natural depression in that rock formation over there? That will be our outdoor amphitheater." He paused. "Can you imagine sitting in an amphithe-ater on that spot, listen-ing to God's Word, sur-rounded by Christian brothers and sisters, all the while looking out over the bay?" Another pause. "I tell you, the Lord is going to use this property to bless many, many people. I'm sure of it."

This property was

Costas clearing land at Porto Astro

the result of much effort and many prayers. For several years Costas had been dreaming and praying about acquiring land for ministry. With the *Morning Star*'s arrival he increased his efforts to find a property. He and young HMU missionary, Bruce McAtee, had spent hours driving together through central and southern Greece, hoping to find a location suitable for Costas's grand vision, but found nothing.

Costas enlisted a real estate agent, outlining his strict criteria: The land must be no more than two hours' drive from Athens, secluded, on the water, with safe mooring for the *Morning Star,* especially protection from strong northerly winds. And, of course, all at an affordable price. It was a tall order, but soon the agent called Costas, excited about a beautiful piece of land for sale just 107 kilometers north of Athens, not far off the National Highway—14.5 acres of seafront property in a beautiful protected bay. Granted, the access road stopped one mile short of the property, so it could be reached only by footpath or boat. This was more seclusion than Costas had asked for. And the price was more than Costas wanted to pay.

But he went to see it. The area was called *Skorponeria,* Greek for "spread-out waters." Years before, a developer had carved roads into the surrounding hillsides, hoping to lure Athenian buyers seeking vacation property. Politics and land-use laws deflated his dreams, and the area sat mostly vacant for decades. This property had long ago been planted as an olive orchard, its many trees now wild and unkempt, barely distinguishable from the natural brush. Development would be difficult, but the long strip of shoreline, the flat lower table, and the upper section with its amazing view made the land ideal for what he had in mind. Costas fell in love with it immediately.

Without Costas's experience and initiative, the lack of a road would have killed the deal. How could one develop property without trucking in supplies? But Costas was undaunted. His jungle experience had taught him that tenacious hard work and creativity could overcome most obstacles. Hadn't he cleared land, built landing strips, and raised schools and clinics in the remote Lakes Plains? This would be easy.

What is more, Costas had navigated jungle rivers, ferrying people and supplies, so he knew water access could help realize the property's potential. A sizable barge or two could carry supplies a mile across the bay, and a few small boats could ferry visitors. And in these waters, if someone fell off a boat, no crocodiles would eat them!

Convenient? Of course not. But *convenience* rarely came into Costas's vocabulary. Very little in Costas's experience had come easy. Rather, the tasks that took the most effort usually provided the richest results. If the Lord confirmed a vision in his heart, he was determined nothing would keep it from completion. No access road? No problem.

Back in Athens he shared with Alky and the kids his growing dreams for the land at Skorponeria. His conviction grew. The new ministry center would host evangelistic and discipleship ministries of all kinds—youth ministry, drug rehabilitation, refugee camps, even an international conference center for outreach into surrounding Slavic and Muslim nations. After a few days of prayer, and approval from the HMU board, he called the realtor. "You've got to get us this property. This is the land God is providing for our ministry."

His resolve was quickly tested. Several members of a family owned the land, and most refused to lower the price. Months of negotiations failed, and Costas was forced to walk away from the table. Nearly a year later, the agent called again. The owners were willing to negotiate, and soon a contract was signed. With the backing of several generous donors, HMU now possessed the beautiful property.

THE RIGHT FAMILY

The next challenge was personnel. Costas believed that God's greatest provision was, not money or material goods, but committed workers. He needed someone to develop the property and live on it during the process. A family would be ideal, but without electricity, running water, or any other conveniences, the property was not welcoming. Any family who could pioneer this ministry would be a rare find.

Thankfully, God specializes in the "impossible." Someone recommended Gary and Margie Rose, currently working at a Christian camp in the mountains of Cyprus. Gary was a wiry Alaskan with skillful hands, an ingenious mind, and a background in construction and road building. Both he and Margie loved living off the land, a lifestyle they were passing on to their two young children, Heather and John. Here was an adventurous family, full of contagious faith, uniquely suited for life in a remote environment.

Costas called the Roses. They were looking for a new ministry assignment, and days later Costas stood with Gary on the Skorponeria beach, sharing his long-term vision. The property became the Roses' new home.

If hospitality were a recognized sport, Margie Rose would be an Olympic champion. During their first year, the family lived in a large nylon tent, made comfortable by their ability to turn little into much. With a few gas burners and an even warmer smile, Margie gained a reputation for greeting visitors with hot tea and freshly baked cakes. Even in the cold and rain their nylon castle stood firm, warmed inside by Gary's wood stove and Margie's nurturing spirit.

Barges were built, and basic equipment was floated in. A couple of small trailer homes were ferried across, improving the family's living conditions. One morning the local fishermen must have wondered if they were dreaming. A seven-ton

JCB earthmover floated across the water. It was no dream. It was just Gary and his visiting father, doing what Alaskans do for fun. They'd constructed a giant barge that perfectly supported the massive machine for its journey across the bay.

Over months and years Costas's vision took shape under Gary's skillful hand. Cisterns were built, culverts and pipes laid, a stone dock constructed, and land cleared. Visiting teams of volunteers cleared fence lines, moved rock, and raised buildings. The old olive orchard came alive, new branches grafted onto the wild trees. Despite the necessary development, the Rose's worked to keep intact the land's natural beauty.

Most significantly, from the Roses' first day the property became a place of effective ministry—a base for launching summer evangelistic campaigns and for the *Morning Star*, as well as a refuge where scores of visiting workers heard the gospel and received personal ministry. Even now Costas's vision was beginning to be realized.

Today, after nearly thirty years' development, the property at Skorponeria—now named Porto Astro—is flourishing. Still inaccessible by road, it receives all supplies—even fresh water—by barge. Yet its remote character adds to its natural beauty. Several buildings now stand where Costas saw them by faith. Cabins, meeting areas, office space, and a commercial kitchen facilitate many camps and retreats throughout the year. Costas was especially gratified when local churches started coming here for retreats and other gatherings, including some memorable baptismal services. Summer sports camps draw youth from around Greece, and camps for refugees expose them to the gospel. The *Morning Star* comes and goes, taking teams to all corners of Greece and the farthest reaches of the Mediterranean.

The young missionary's question had been a simple one. "Costas, what do you see?" With eyes of faith, Costas had seen it all. His dream is still taking shape.

Land cleared at Porto Astro, as seen from across the bay

Costas leading a baptism ceremony at the property

CHAPTER 29

HELLAS 2002

The 1990s were closing, a new millennium about to dawn. Costas reflected gratefully on all God had done through HMU over twenty years.

- A dynamic team of foreign missionaries had been established, as well as short- and medium-term workers who contributed significantly.

- Scores of Greek young people had been discipled and trained in ministry, many going on to work in their churches.

- Summer campaigns continued to spread the good news throughout Greece.

- The *Morning Star* sailed on regular evangelistic trips, ferrying teams to islands large and small, now with Costas's fourth son, Alex, as skipper.

- The ministry at Porto Astro grew and hosted a steady stream of workers and equipment.

- A growing refugee ministry served Middle-Easterners landing in Athens by the tens of thousands, most viewing Greece as a stepping stone to North America or Northern Europe.

Costas had been blessed on the home front as well. The Macris kids were grown with families and ministries of their own. Johnathan and his wife, Miriam (Raney), were missionaries with HMU; Haris, now a medical doctor, pursued medical missions with his wife, Maria (Moschovis); Neal and his wife, Jenny (Baldwin), worked with Greater Europe Mission as church planters in northern Athens; and Alex and JoAnne (Luesink) led the expanding work of the *Morning Star*. The Macris girls were active in the Lord's work, Ifie and her husband, Calvin Janzen, deeply involved with their church in Canada, and Manon and her husband, Stephanos Michalios, in Chicago pursuing advanced degrees in Christian education.

Alky and Costas were proud of their children, grateful that most lived in Greece. Of course, the many grandchildren were precious gifts that sweetened life.

This was a rich season, and many might be tempted to slow their pace and ease into life's final chapters. This prospect held no attraction for Costas. Retirement came the other side of heaven's gates, not before. His body was growing tired and often refused to comply with his robust vision, but he continued to push his endurance to the limit.

So when a thirty-something Greek-Australian named Jim Bellas visited Athens with a grand vision, Costas took time to listen. Jim was bothered that so few of his fellow Greeks had a born-again experience. Jim had given his life to Christ as a boy in Australia. His grandfather, Nick Lootaris, had helped establish the evangelical work in Australia. Now, traveling the land of his forefathers, Jim was saddened by the spiritual state of his Greek compatriots. He longed to help Greeks around the world understand this country's spiritual needs. Why not convene a conference for Greek Christians from all nations, to develop their vision for the land of their fathers? Some might return as missionaries. Others would give and pray.

Costas listened politely and at first remained uncommitted. The HMU team was growing and busy. But Jim's vision refused to fade. Costas, a dreamer himself, knew what it was to carry a burden others couldn't yet grasp. Finally, determined to not stand in God's way, Costas pledged his support. He and the mission would help Jim with his conference.

To capitalize on the turn of the millennium, they originally planned toward the year 2000. But this proved unrealistic, so they pushed back to 2002. Thus Hellas 2002 was born. (*Hellas* is the ancient word for Greece.) This effort would consume much of the mission's energy for two years.

First they chose the conference venue, a seaside resort hotel just south of Athens. The facility needed repair, and the rental agreement required the mission to paint its exterior. Countless man hours went into painting, fixing, and decorating the hotel. As usual, Costas's eye for detail and beauty took him the extra mile to prepare an inviting venue. Jim Bellas, HMU missionaries and staff, and many volunteers from different countries worked together. Five months before the conference, Costas invested himself full-time. Drawing upon his reputation among Greek communities around the world, he wrote countless letters, personally inviting people to come for this historic occasion.

The June conference drew nearly four hundred Greek participants from more than fourteen countries. For five days they worshipped together and heard Greek pastors and leaders teach from God's Word. More than thirty speakers led keynote sessions and workshops, all centered on the spiritual life and the needs of Greece. George Verwer, director of the well-known international organization Operation

Mobilization, was the main speaker. This was coordinated with a special Youth Fest near the sea and a choir festival in downtown Athens featuring special guest Paul Kotzopoulous, a world-renowned pianist.

Attendees viewed ministry displays and connected with others interested in sharing Christ with the Greek people. They were encouraged to pray, give, and come serve, if the Lord so led. Costas challenged the attendees to consider missions carefully, as something "close to the heart of God."

Costas and Johnathan Macris leading a session at Hellas 2002

Hellas 2002 was the first such international congress in Greece, and by all accounts was a resounding success. Participants returned to their countries with a fresh picture of God's working in Greece. Jim Bellas's dream had come true, due not only to hard work, but also to the more than one hundred prayer cells in thirty-plus countries that had prayed for the event.

Costas was thrilled, but the effort took a toll on his health. Prior to the conference he had become increasingly exhausted. He had often slept on his office couch, and he sometimes fell asleep during meetings and phone calls. Costas had always been most energized when busy about the Lord's work, no matter how tired his body. Alky had grown used to this but was constantly concerned about his health. She tried to get him to slow down, and sometimes he acquiesced, but only for a season.

After the conference Costas initiated a search for his

replacement as HMU president. When the board recommended his son Johnathan, Costas was hesitant. He didn't want to be seen as playing favorites. The board insisted, and Costas finally agreed. Johnathan was uniquely prepared for the task, having inherited his father's broad shoulders and dynamic faith. A natural passing of the baton took place, and the ensuing transition was smooth. The board also voted to change HMU's international name to Hellenic Ministries (HM), which better summarized the mission and its objective.

The change of role by no means meant slowing down for Costas, but it did mean a significant shift in his responsibilities. After eight fruitful years the Rose family had moved on from Porto Astro—the Skorponeria property—to other ministry. Now that a basic infrastructure had been established, Costas found himself drawn to Porto Astro's serenity more often. Balancing the demands of HM's Athens office, he was already devoting more of his energies to the coastal property.

This occupation brought Costas physical renewal. He also discovered new creativity while shaping the land. As he'd done years before in the faraway jungles, he built rock walls and stone paths and planted flowers wherever he could. He had inherited his father's love for beauty and attention to detail. He imagined himself an architect of nature, doing in the wild what his father had done with buildings and pavilions. His personal ministry to teams and discipleship of refugee workers made this season all the more profitable. He worked closely with two Albanian men, Arturo and Hamza and their families, who had fled to Greece for a better life. They were skilled and willing workers, and Costas spent hours igniting in them a passion for the Bible, eventually leading them to faith in Christ.

But neither he nor the rest of the staff could ignore HM's other ongoing efforts. Summer campaigns continued each year, and 2003 was when they introduced summer youth camps at Porto Astro. For two glorious weeks under the August sun more than one hundred teenagers enjoyed a diet of sports, singing, and teaching from God's Word. They spent their days on water skis, inner tubes, wind surfers, and speedboats. They climbed rocks, shot archery, played soccer, and trampolined. And they received a clear call to commitment to Christ and His cause.

HM excelled at dreaming up ways to take the gospel to the Greek people. After more than twenty summer campaigns, Costas and the team were ready for a new challenge, and the following summer it came, when the world's focus would once again be on the small nation of Greece.

CHAPTER 30

THE ISLANDS
REJOICE

In the summer of 2004, the nations came to Athens. It was Greece's turn to host the Summer Olympic Games. Dozens of international Christian organizations planned coordinated outreach efforts, and HM helped as best they could. A number of Greek churches and local Christian movements also joined hands under the title "More than Gold," using the Olympics as a platform for the gospel.

The Hellenic Ministries team prayerfully sensed God leading in an unusual direction. During the Olympics many Athenians planned to escape the city for outlying villages and islands, many renting out their homes. HM's two decades of summer evangelistic campaigns had touched nearly every mainland region. The eighty inhabited islands, however, had received little attention except through the *Morning Star*'s small teams. Why not take the gospel to the Greek islands? During the Olympics they could reach both the inhabitants and many vacationing Athenians.

Operation Gideon (OG), as the effort became known, envisioned small teams simultaneously sharing about Jesus on many larger islands. The format would be simple: Each island team would divide nine days into thirds—the first three days in prayer and fasting, the second three distributing literature, and the last three proclaiming the gospel.

Dates were set and brochures printed. Many Greek volunteers caught the vision and helped at the office. Short-term workers came from other countries. HM's full-time staff, already stretched to capacity with existing responsibilities, still took up the challenge. Operation Gideon would be HM's largest outreach to date.

In August 2004, while athletes and spectators converged on newly refreshed Athens and its gleaming Olympic venues, three hundred Operation Gideon participants contended on a different front. They convened at a large warehouse in the heart of the city, laboriously converted into "Hospitality Village." Here members gathered into teams, slept on cots and sleeping bags, and enjoyed four days of Bible teaching, training, and worship before heading to their island assignments. Atlanta-area pastor Peter Grant challenged participants to exercise the faith of Gideon—to trust that a big God can use small teams to accomplish mighty things. They even enjoyed an open-air concert by the Christian band Delirious in one of the city's main squares. Many countries were represented, a sweet foretaste of heaven. Finally, thirty-seven teams embarked on island ferries, hearts full of faith and anticipation.

Most island tourists that summer arrived with expectations of picture-perfect sunsets, attracted by iconic images from Santorini, Kos, Rhodes, and Mykonos, with their white-washed villages and translucent seas. But for nine days the OG teams saw these islands through different eyes. They fasted and prayed, standing over seaside villages with outstretched hands. They walked cobbled streets and whitewashed alleyways, hanging bags with Bibles and literature on every available doorknob. Then they sang songs, performed pantomime, or drew pictures on sketch boards—anything to attract notice and share about Jesus.

On the tenth day they regathered at Hospitality Village with more stories than anyone could count, full of joy and electric worship. Many teams recounted life-changing receptions of the message about Jesus. One team had led twenty-six people in prayer for salvation. Others told of divine opportunities they could never have anticipated. They'd built many relationships, and many people had willingly accepted Bibles. God had obviously gone before them. The teams rejoiced in His presence and power.

They had also encountered opposition. The locals were accustomed to hordes of drunken, offensive tourists. But teams of smiling people passing out Bibles? Now here was something new. Most Greeks responded with curiosity, friendliness, or indifference, but some—including the Orthodox hierarchy—took offense at the intrusion and made their displeasure clear. A bishop on one of the larger islands distributed a letter:

Dear Christians,

A few days ago an organization which is foreign to our Orthodox Christian belief, called Hellenic Ministries, came and distributed packages to homes around_____ and probably to other islands as well. The material they are distributing is Protestant in nature and totally against our Orthodox Christian belief. For example, they deny the sacraments of the church, and they don't give honor to our saints, and they try to mislead you with offers of New Testament books and messages. We would like to warn you as Orthodox Christians not to have any relationship with these heretics, and don't give any attention to the gifts they are offering.

Office of the Metropolitan Bishop

Yet, in spite of some hostile reception, the operation was so successful that Costas and the HM team decided to repeat the island outreach two years later. In July 2006 hundreds of participants from around the world would again gather to reach the Greek islands. "Operation Gideon II" would launch from Porto Astro, rather than Hospitality Village.

In preparation, Costas doubled his efforts preparing the seacoast property, grateful for the help of Paul and Kathryn Kline, the Macrises' dear coworkers from Irian Jaya, now working full-time in Greece. Paul's mechanical aptitude and Kathryn's attention to detail strongly served Costas's vision.

In typical HM style, Operation Gideon II required all hands on deck. HM missionaries—short- and long-term— helped prepare the property. They added rock walls, flowers, and decorative greenery. They stretched massive canopies for shade over meeting areas and leveled tent sites. Porto Astro had never looked better.

By every measure, the second Operation Gideon proved as successful as the first. Costas couldn't help thanking God for

Participants of Operation Gideon II gathered at Porto Astro

all He had done. On the last night of the program, he rejoiced as many Greek young people dedicated themselves to the Lord and His service. Here was the culmination of so many ministry dreams for his beloved Greece.

He sat with Alky, watching the sun dissolve red into Skorponeria Bay, the masts of the Morning Star silhouetted, straight and tall, against the darkening sky. It seemed only yesterday that he'd received Don Stephens' call, and he smiled at the memory of Ken Overman and crew on their odyssey across the Atlantic. Now the *Morning Star* was here, taking God's word to the inhabited islands of Greece.

His eyes traced the property's outline, from the pebbly beach to the captain's quarters and outbuildings, to the commercial kitchen, and beyond to the guest cabins. He saw the climbing tower and the soccer field. He took stock of the many rock walls, iron railings, and cement footpaths and patios that now welcomed visitors.

His mind traveled back in time to faraway Kanggime, Ninia, and Taiyeve, to the gradual taming of the wild terrain, the hard work that had converted youthful energy into effective ministry. Such a satisfying labor of love. Now he admired Porto Astro, and he rejoiced at the peaceful spirit of unity so obviously present.

Costas turned his attention to the teams as they shared their island stories. Here were hundreds of faithful brothers and sisters—Greeks and many other nationalities—all intent on reaching his beloved country with Christ's love. Their wholehearted service humbled him. *Surely, this is God's hour for Greece,* he thought.

He looked warmly at Alky, then at his adult children, several of whom were leading the evening program. He watched as they worshiped and gave public witness of God's faithfulness. He smiled at his grandbabies, bounced on grownup knees.

He could not be more proud. And he was very tired.

CHAPTER 31

"PEARLS AROUND MY NECK"

Costas grew noticeably weaker after Operation Gideon II. He wasn't in pain, just lacking the energy that had always been his ally.

He had been keeping a secret. A year earlier, tests in Chicago had revealed new cancer. Knowing that was likely his last chance to visit many supporters, he extended the North America trip. Now, twelve months later, additional testing indicated the cancer had grown. So Costas and Alky traveled in late September 2006 to St. Luke's Hospital in Thessaloniki for more biopsies. Dr. Katsarkas, Costas's close friend and director of the hospital, broke the difficult news. Cancer had likely spread throughout his body.

Immediate surgery was scheduled, and a large tumor blocking the large intestine was removed. The postsurgery report was encouraging: The cancer appeared to be localized and may have been contained. The surgeon had tried to remove lymph nodes in the area for further testing, but found none—apparently removed seventeen years earlier in St. Louis.

But four days later Costas was still bleeding from the surgery. He was so weak that he couldn't talk. A second surgery found diffused hemorrhaging—internal bleeding from multiple locations. His life was ebbing away.

Then he stabilized. The following day his blood pressure returned to normal, the bleeding stopped, and all tubes were removed. For the first time in days Costas became coherent and looked better. Soon he was sitting in a chair and drinking tea.

Alky and the kids breathed sighs of relief. Most of the family had come to the hospital, and a few were waiting on standby for flights from North America. Notes, phone calls, and e-mails had begun pouring in from around the globe. It seemed the Lord was again pleased to answer His people's many requests for Costas's healing.

But the improvement was short-lived, and Costas took another turn for the worse. Acute abdominal pain required a third surgery, which found part of his small intestine dying and his liver beginning to fail. His breathing became difficult, and he was once again intubated.

Johnathan recalls his thoughts as he flew into Thessaloniki on a 737:

How I long to commend him for an awesome job, winning the race set before him here. I want to hold his face and tell him thank you one last time. Yet Dad just might surprise us yet. On the other hand, I think the angels are applauding pretty hard in the heavenly grandstands. They know he's closing on the finish line. Could it be that they are anxious for him to come on home to rest, so they too can catch their breath?

Deep down inside and through the eyes of my heart, I see Jesus at the other side of the line smiling, ready to welcome his sprinter son home with a "well done" wreath of honor in his outstretched, nail-scarred hands. I'm left to wonder if heaven is winning out this time. All we can do is wait and see.

On the twelfth day the family was put on notice and gathered around Costas's bed. These were difficult, precious moments for this hurting, triumphant family. The kids spoke lovingly into their dad's ear. They prayed with him and stroked his hair, sometimes laughing together over memories, sometimes weeping. Some rubbed his feet, remembering the Lord's blessing: "How beautiful on the mountains are the feet of the messenger who brings good news, the good news of peace and salvation, the news that the God of Israel reigns!" (Isaiah 52:7, NLT).

When visiting hours ended, Alky and the children found their way to the hospital dining room and ordered. Someone remembered aloud how they would sing together, before a meal, in family worship, or during a music night. A song broke out around the table, and for thirty minutes the rest of the dining room looked on while Alky and the kids sang familiar hymns and choruses, sweet harmony accentuated with tears. They ended with one of Costas's favorite choruses, "Bless the Lord, Oh My Soul." This was a beautiful moment of remembrance and release, a tribute to their precious daddy, who would soon be singing with angels.

The Macris children's obvious love for their parents touched many hospital employees. When a nurse mentioned this to Costas, he smiled. "My children are like pearls around my neck." One employee approached Alky. "I want you to know that I am Orthodox, but when I die, I hope my children will love me the same way your children love their father."

Costas remained another week in the ICU, suspended between heaven and earth. At times he seemed to improve, but always followed by decline. Alky remained at Costas's side. Her children brought her strength, but sometimes she found herself alone. Once she was feeling quite discouraged, when a family friend appeared with bags of cookies and sweets. On another occasion Costas's brother lifted her spirits. These and others accompanied her through a dark, lonely valley.

By mid-October Costas's body was clearly failing. In his children's words, it was time for this warrior to lay down his arms. The entire family said their earthly farewells, and that afternoon Costas slipped through the veil to his eternal reward, Johnathan holding his father's hand.

A few hours later, Johnathan wrote a short note to family friends and supporters:

> *He Won!*
> My dearest friends and family, and to all who knew and loved my father, Costas Macris:
> My sweet, sweet daddy finished the race and won! Daddy stepped over the finish line at *12:40 p.m., Wednesday, October 18, two days after my birthday.* He gave all he had in this life to gain the victor's crown of righteousness and eternity with Jesus! *[emphasis Johnathan's]*

CELEBRATION

Five days later, on October 23, a crowd of nearly a thousand gathered at Athens's First Evangelical Church to remember this man of faith. Friends came from all corners of Greece and around the world to honor a man who had touched their lives by personal relationship or by force of example. A powerful voice of the Greek evangelical community had gone home, and the historic church overflowed.

Costas had asked the family to wear bright colors, for he wanted his service to be a celebration. Alky compromised and wore gray, her heart too heavy for festivity.

Christian leaders talked about Costas's outsized influence on their walks with Christ. Many had entered ministry because of his encouragement and example. Then Dr. Katsarkas gave a moving tribute and shared from the Scriptures.

The lights lowered for a photo montage, and Alky relived a lifetime of memories. First came pictures of the newly married couple, then their first days in the jungle. Slide by slide, the substance of her life was revealed, from first-term station-sitting to the Lakes Plains to the sickness that led to St. Louis. Then to Greece and the founding of HMU. She saw the 1980s trial, the *Morning Star,* the summer campaigns, Porto Astro, and more—a kaleidoscope of experiences. Oh, how the years had flown.

The last slide was of Costas, his six children and nineteen grandchildren—almost too much for Alky to bear. She felt gratitude mixed with tremendous loss. How would she survive without her Costas?

She felt a cloud of depression settling over her—something she hadn't experienced for years. More speakers spoke, but the darkness grew. Then HM missionary Bruce McAtee got up to sing. Costas had always loved Bruce's singing, and as the song began, Alky felt her spirit lift. "Thank You for Giving to the Lord" reached its finale. She felt the depression dissipate completely, never to return, as if the Lord had spoken the words of Bruce's song directly to her heart.

Finally the Macris children each shared about their dad. Haris talked about his dad's strict discipline and loving concern. Ifie spoke of her dad's affection and how he would tenderly place his cheek on hers. She also remembered his grateful attitude, even for difficulties. Manon talked of her parents' enduring hospitality and how her dad would invite strangers to their house if they needed a meal or a place to stay. Alex remembered spankings and his gratitude for his father's loving discipline. Neil, with typical evangelistic zeal, reminded the audience of his dad's love for the gospel. He shared the plan of salvation and invited listeners to receive Christ as Savior. "If you want to see Costas again, you must surrender your life to the Lord."

Finally Johnathan spoke of his father's love for the Greek people. He challenged the audience to continue the legacy by following in his dad's ministry footsteps. Then Alky, with children and grandchildren, sang a chorus to end the service—their unified shout of triumph. Because of Jesus, death's sting was overcome. Because of Jesus, their Costas was more alive than ever!

The Macris family at Costas's burial.
L to R: Johnathan, Neil, Ifie, Alky, Manon, Alex, Haris.

CHAPTER 32

LESSONS FROM A LIFE OF FAITH

Don and Carlene Schlemeier, a young Midwestern couple with hearts for God and interest in world missions, sat in St. Louis's Hope Church, enjoying the spring 1962 missions conference. They watched a young missionary couple approach the stage. Carlene's heart warmed when she saw the Greek woman, introduced as Alky Macris, cradling a sleeping five-month-old boy. Many missionaries were introduced that evening, but Carlene was especially drawn to this couple's story. Similar in age, she was curious about their journey and in which part of the world they would soon be serving.

Alky's charismatic husband, Costas, began his presentation about their impending move to the jungles of Irian Jaya. A slideshow displayed the harsh jungle conditions, villages of grass huts, a culture untouched by the modern world. Dark-skinned tribesmen, nearly naked and glistening with paint and pig fat, filled the screen. To the Schlemeiers, this might be a scene from a distant planet. Yet Costas talked with enthusiasm about the successful work already underway in the interior highlands. He then spoke of the many tribes who had not yet heard the gospel, and of his and Alky's desire to reach them for Christ.

Don and Carlene sat in reflective silence. They admired the Macrises' willingness to live in such harsh conditions, but couldn't imagine taking a baby to such a place. They drove home sharing how their hearts were moved. They knew the young family would need help. Somehow, they agreed together, God was asking them to assist in the Macrises' endeavor.

Don wrote to Costas, saying that he and Carlene wanted to help. They couldn't give much financially, at least not yet, but they promised to pray and assist the work as they were able. They were delighted to receive a response. Costas graciously thanked them for their prayer and their interest.

Thus began a cooperative effort that lasted more than forty years. Though the Schlemeiers would later move to Washington State, their prayer and support for the Macris family never wavered. They organized prayer groups, wrote encouraging letters, sent care packages and supplies, and made friends and neighbors aware of the Macrises' ministry. They facilitated the Macrises' visits on furlough. During Costas's trial in Athens they organized letter-writing campaigns to the Greek government and to Greek embassies in the United States. They played a key role in the material and spiritual supply chain that kept the Macris family on the front lines. Costas and Alky attracted many such supporters, without whom the work would not have happened.

After Costas's funeral, Don reflected in a letter on what he'd learned from Costas over the years. Don's experience is hardly unique, for many felt Costas's influence. A summary of Don's list helps us reflect on the qualities that made Costas such a servant of God:

A MAN DEEPLY IMPACTED BY JESUS CHRIST

From the moment he prayed to receive Christ as his Savior, Costas's life was radically changed. Jesus took hold of his heart, his dreams, and his energies so completely that everything else paled in comparison. This was no passing emotional experience. Costas knew he had been carried from spiritual darkness into life-giving light, and he wanted everyone—everywhere—to experience this same freedom.

One of Costas's great burdens was that his countrymen—mostly Orthodox—would come to this same assurance of faith in Christ. He was careful not to equate church affiliation with personal faith, for a number of Orthodox friends were clearly born-again believers in Christ. The majority, however, revered God and the church and tried in some way to be "religious" but had never been taught to read and understand the Scriptures for themselves, or to know God in a personal, life-transforming manner.

If all of Costas's many activities were to be boiled down, all his visions dissected, all his programs, efforts, and energies ultimately explained, this would be the distillation of his heart and actions: that men and women might come to faith in Christ for the forgiveness of their sins, and thus live for and enjoy God forever. For Costas, life had no greater purpose.

A MAN OF EXTRAORDINARY FAITH

Those who knew Costas were often amazed at his childlike faith. Jesus spoke highly of those who trust the Father with the simple faith of a child, and this trait set Costas apart.

Was God who He claimed to be in His Word? Costas believed so, and he carried this belief to its ultimate conclusion. He believed unswervingly in God's sovereignty, which fueled the confidence to trust his heavenly Father in all things.

He could move his young family to the jungles, he could dare to face down tribesmen with bows and arrows, he could face a jail sentence of three and a half years—all because he had complete confidence in the goodness of God in all things.

Don Schlemeier was impacted by Costas's ability to trust God, even in dire circumstances. If God closed a door, Costas learned to test the windows, so as not to miss God's plan. He sought to trust God in everything—even difficult things like cancer—knowing that all would serve God's glory. He believed nothing could harm him that God did not allow for His purposes.

This childlike ability to trust propelled Costas to make requests of God that most wouldn't consider. Why not? If God parted the Red Sea, could He not provide an airplane or two? If God stopped the sun, can't He perform miracles today? Costas believed God could do great things—and often would—if asked in simple trust.

A MAN OF GREAT VISION

Costas was born a visionary. He saw what others could not, which sometimes put him at odds with those of a more practical bent. When he initially floated Regions Wings, good reasoning caused doubts. The difficulties were enough to make a mission executive's head spin. When Costas pressed for open-air evangelism in Greece, many pushed back. But in both cases Costas's visionary instincts proved reliable. Over time he learned the skill of bringing people with him as he moved an idea forward.

RBMU director Joe Conley remembers his first encounter with Costas at the Pennsylvania mission headquarters:

Elberon Avenue lay in a deep freeze, the street robed in solid ice. Costas was heading for Irian Jaya, and as I helped him load his drums of personal effects onto the truck that would take him to the Philadelphia docks, he could not restrain himself telling me of the steamboat he would buy to evangelize the great Frederick Hendricks Island off the southeast coast of West Irian. He never did, but Costas always thought in Calebesque terms![13]

Costas could also speak vision into the lives of others. Costas readily listened to others' new ministry ideas. But then he would also challenge them to carry it through. He believed every Christian should be encouraged toward that which God had put in their heart. The evangelical community in Greece was small, so he was quick to help speakers and musicians find ways to express their gifting.

Costas often helped people see about themselves what they hadn't seen before. George Athanasakis, husband of Costas's long-time secretary, Marina, remembers accompanying Costas for a weekend ministry event. At the ripe old age of twenty-four, George spoke to the church's youth that Friday evening, for which he'd prepared. The next afternoon Costas asked him to preach the Sunday morning sermon. George was terrified but reluctantly agreed. The following day George stood behind the church's large pulpit and he opened his mouth to begin. A tiny squeak came out. But he pressed ahead, and under Costas's approving smile he finished. Today George travels throughout Greece, preaching regularly in churches. Costas helped him, and many others, enter into ministry.

A MAN OF BOUNDLESS ENERGY

Costas was a blur of activity. The reputation he gained as a young missionary, he retained most of his life. Costas loved to work, naturally bent toward perpetual activity. He was driven by the belief that God had given him a job and limited time to accomplish it. Having survived tropical illnesses, cancer, and numerous surgeries, he harbored no illusions about life's brevity. His martyred friends also served to eradicate complacency.

Costas had a love-hate relationship with sleep. He enjoyed a good night's rest, but sleep could get in the way of work. Often his desk lamp stayed lit until two or three a.m. for letter writing, even after a full day's work.

Occasional sleep deprivation resulted in legendary tales, as when Costas fell asleep on his motorbike at a traffic light. He often struggled to stay awake through afternoon meetings and uneventful phone calls. He justified this with a wink to one of his kids during a Sunday morning church service. He leaned close and pointed to a verse in which the apostle Paul wrote of his many sleepless nights (2 Corinthians 11:27). "See, it's biblical!" he whispered with feigned enlightenment.

A MAN WHO LOVED HIS WIFE AND CHILDREN

One might think, given Costas's drive, that Alky and the children would have felt neglected. This was never the case. Anyone privileged to spend time in the Macris home can attest to the extraordinary quality of their family life. Alky was the hub, around which all else moved. Her steady, nurturing presence grounded the home's frenetic energy. In good Greek tradition, her skill in the home and kitchen set a scene in which ministry and politics could be debated, fueled by an abundance of olive oil, feta, and love.

If Alky set the stage, Costas directed the show, but with an amazing ability to engage his children. The home could be strict, but also fun, and Costas made time for jokes, singing, and laughter. They played games and acted silly together. Their hospitality was second to none.

Costas refused to keep his work and family separate. He included each family member in the mission's work. The Macris kids grew up knowing the value of hard work, but work for a purpose: to make Jesus known. On summer campaign or for a Monday evening program at Evripidou Hall, each child—at any age—had a job that made a genuine contribution. It's no wonder the Macris children are all doing ministry to this day.

A MAN WHO LOVED PEOPLE

Costas would often go out of his way to help a person in need or to invite someone home for a hot meal or a place to sleep. One Christmas Day, when the family had finished eating at a downtown restaurant, they saw an elderly gentleman who appeared lost. Costas approached and noticed the man's confusion, so he invited him to spend Christmas afternoon with them. Over cookies and tea, the man filled their living room with his adventures in the Second World War. Later Costas helped him find the senior home where he lived.

Alky's aging parents needed special care, so Costas insisted they live in the Macris home. He bought a hospital bed and nursed them until their heaven-going.

A friend remembers Costas's many trips to the hospital to care for a relative. A coworker in Irian talks of the anonymous donation that helped him begin a new ministry, funds he eventually traced back to Costas. When a young husband, a family friend, wanted to learn computer skills, Costas bought him a new computer. A Bible school student admired Costas's tie and was shocked to receive it as a gift on the spot. A young boy expressed interest in missions, then unexpectedly began receiving two missionary magazines.

Costas extended himself for the sake of others. This, combined with his abounding faith and energy, made him a strong force for good in many lives.

A MAN WITH FLAWS

Lest we seem to be nominating our friend for sainthood (something Costas would be first to refuse!), a full picture of the man admits to weaker qualities.

Costas could be difficult to work with, due to his incessant drive and his visionary gifting. Even strong young men and women struggled to keep up.

Costas could be stubborn—a positive trait in the face of spiritual opposition. But stubbornness sometimes fostered an unteachable spirit. Still, he was usually quick to make things right.

Theodoris Kalogeropoulos, a family friend and ministry partner, remembers that for summer campaigns Costas would often lead the large caravan of vehicles from village to village. But his sense of direction was not always reliable. The drivers behind him, who read the signs and knew the way, would mutter, "No, Costas, don't turn left. Don't turn left." Sure enough, Costas—often deep in conversation—would turn left, even against Alky's suggestions. The long caravan of vehicles would follow like a giant caterpillar winding through the countryside, eventually correcting course in a group U-turn.

Few would accuse Costas of outright character deficiencies. Disagreements usually came down to a difference in vision or philosophy. Though some disagreed with Costas's progressive style, few would impugn his motives. The respect of his coworkers and countrymen is an enduring part of his legacy.

*   *   *

As family and close friends gathered at Athens's prestigious First Cemetery to lay Costas's body to rest that October day, an older Greek woman, there for some other purpose, couldn't help noticing the large gathering. She placed flowers on her son's nearby grave and overheard the affirming comments. When the crowd broke into joyful song, her curiosity was piqued.

The short ceremony ended, and the crowd dispersed. She grabbed someone's arm, leaned in, and said, "I heard the many nice things being said about this person. He must have been a great man."

From Greece to Indonesia and around the world, untold numbers of people can only agree. Costas Macris was indeed a great man, an enduring example of wholehearted devotion to the Greatest One of all—his Lord and Savior, Jesus Christ.

AFTERWORD

by Johnathan Macris
President of Hellenic Ministries

I leaned forward in the small camp chair and planted my face in my hands, shaking my head at Dad's words. *Oh no, not again.* I smiled. *Not another dream, another fanciful idea, way beyond reality, disconnected from logical pragmatism.*

I lifted my eyes and covertly observed others sitting around me, wondering what they were thinking. I'd asked my dad to say a few words to close our meeting, but I wasn't ready for what I was hearing. Weren't our resources—and our faith—already stretched to the limit?

It was summer 2006, and our entire HM team had gathered at Porto Astro for a day of prayer and preparation. We were weeks away from welcoming nearly three hundred volunteers for Operation Gideon II, during which thirty thousand Bibles would be distributed on forty Greek islands in the Mediterranean and Aegean Seas. This would complete our vision of placing a Bible in every home on eighty inhabited islands, symbolically surrounding Greece with the gospel and a testimony of God's love.

Our team was already stretched to the limit. We were short of finances, volunteers, and, to be honest, stamina, with a thousand logistical puzzles yet to be solved. But Dad poured out his heart on that summer evening, dropping a visionary bombshell that shook our team. With conviction he challenged us not to stop with the islands, but to see that every home in every village in Greece receive the Scriptures as well!

This was when I buried my face in my hands. I could count

to eighty—the number of Greece's inhabited islands—but the mainland was a different reality. This would mean door-to-door distribution in upwards of ten thousand villages! Truly this was a Costas-sized vision.

Looking back, I'm glad I didn't cut my dad short and end our meeting on time. Little did I know this would be the last time my father would challenge our mission team and encourage us from God's Word. Just two months later he was admitted to St. Luke's hospital in Thessaloniki, never to return to his Athens home and ministry.

Dad had lived two lives, one to reach the indigenous tribes of Irian Jaya, and now he was intent on reaching all of his beloved homeland, Greece, with the gospel.

In 2009 my brother Neil was the first of the Macris siblings to return to the hot, steamy tropics where we grew up. As his plane landed at Taijeve, now nearly abandoned and almost completely reclaimed by the jungle, Neil couldn't hide his disappointment. But before the propeller had fully stopped, someone pulled open the door, and Neil found himself literally carried to meet the large crowd joyfully waiting to greet the only returning Macris in nearly forty years.

During the meeting that followed, an older tribesman turned to Neil with awe and said, "Don't feel bad for the buildings that your dad built on this station. Yes, they are decaying. But you need to know that the gospel your

Neil Macris being greeted by church leaders at Karubaga, including Otto Kobak, the grandson of the warrior who shot at Costas with an arrow

dad brought us so many years ago is flowing through these jungles like our mighty rivers."

How grateful we are that Mom and Dad's legacy lives on, both in Indonesia and in Greece. As a family we desire to honor the Lord by continuing the work they so joyfully began.

As for that small matter of distributing more Bibles? Once again it was a vision only Dad could foresee. By God's grace, after ten summers of hard work, with the help of thousands of volunteers from around the world, this July we hope to celebrate the delivery of more than one million Bibles to over one million Greek homes!

In many ways it seems the work in Greece has just begun. Hellenic Ministries has established a variety of ministries, all with the intent of reaching Greece and the surrounding countries with the life-changing message of Jesus Christ. We'd be honored if you would pray for us. Better yet, why not come and join us? Information on short- and long-term opportunities is available at www.HellenicMinistries.org.

Above all, our prayer is that you sense the wonder and awe of God, and then seek to pursue and serve Him with all your heart, mind, and soul. Your life is worth living beyond the span of one lifetime. As Dad modeled so well, if you grasp your life close to yourself, you stand to lose it all. But if you passionately give yourself to Christ and to others, you too can live an extraordinary life.

JOHNATHAN MACRIS
December 2016
Athens, Greece

APPENDIX:
WHAT COSTAS WOULD WANT YOU TO KNOW

by Tom Mahairas, pastor of Manhattan Bible Church, founder of CitiVision

My wife, Vicky, and I were raised in the sex, drugs, and rock music lifestyle of the 1960s. Then someone shared the gospel with us, we become believers, and eventually we started a church in New York City.

As a young pastor, I was asked to speak at a Greek Bible conference in summer 1974, in upstate New York. That weekend we met Costas and Alky for the first time. As they shared about their ministry to the people of Irian Jaya, we were profoundly impacted. They exuded a faith and confidence we had never witnessed. Costas's spirit of joy was infectious. Alky had a glow of peace and kindness. Here was a Greek missionary couple on fire for God. They had taken the words of Jesus literally and were laying down their lives for His sake (see Luke 9:23).

For the next thirty years our church supported them, and I came to know Costas well. In fact, he became to me a spiritual father and a mentor. For this reason I could share many stories about Costas. I could tell you about his extreme generosity. I could also share the many ways he denied himself to bring unity and blessing to the body of Christ. Yet the greatest thing I can share about Costas is that he loved Jesus, and he was determined to share this love with everyone.

Let me close this book with one final message that, I believe, Costas would most want you to know:

COSTAS WOULD WANT YOU TO KNOW THAT GOD LOVES YOU

God loves everyone, even you and me, and He sent Jesus to die for each of us. This is the biggest truth in the world and in the Word. The greatest passage in the Bible is:

> For God so loved the world, that He gave His only begotten Son, that whoever believes in Him shall not perish, but have eternal life. For God did not send the Son into the world to judge the world, but that the world might be saved through Him. (John 3:16–17)

This passage reveals:

- The greatest love: "God so loved the world."
- The greatest gift: "that He gave His only begotten Son."
- The greatest offer: "that whoever believes in Him."
- The greatest escape: "should not perish."
- The greatest relationship and promise: "but have eternal life."

COSTAS WOULD WANT YOU TO KNOW THAT JESUS CHRIST DIED FOR YOU

Even though we have all broken God's heart and commandments, He still loves us and provided a way for us to begin a personal relationship with Him. The Bible says,

> While we were still helpless, at the right time Christ died for the ungodly. . . . But God demonstrates His own love toward us, in that while we were yet sinners, Christ died for us. (Romans 5:6–8)

Jesus said, "I am the way, and the truth, and the life; no man comes to the Father but through Me" (John 14:6).

COSTAS WOULD DESIRE THAT YOU PUT YOUR TRUST IN CHRIST AND BE SAVED

It is not through our own self-effort and good works that we can go to heaven. There is no spiritual scale that weighs our good against our bad, for this would be "us-doing." Rather, Jesus said it was finished on the cross—the work has been done by Him.

> As many as received Him, to them He gave the right to become children of God, even to those who believe in His name, who were born, not of blood nor of the will of the flesh nor of the will of man, but of God. (John 1:12–13)

> We are born . . .

- "Not of blood" = not of racial or ethnic heritage—that is, Relatives.
- "Nor of the will of the flesh" = not of personal desire—that is, Resolutions.
- "Nor of the will of man" = not of manmade systems—that is, Religions.

Religion places our focus on good works and righteous deeds. Good works are important, but they will never save us. Only by placing our trust in Christ, and in His payment on the cross for our sins, can anyone be saved. The Bible is clear:

> By grace you have been saved through faith; and that not of yourselves, it is the gift of God; not as a result of works, so that no one may boast. (Ephesians 2:8–9)

If we humbly confess our sin and trust Jesus Christ to forgive us, He promises to do so and to cleanse us from all unrighteousness (see 1 John 1:9).

If you truly desire to trust Christ for salvation and to commit your life to Him, you can use this simple prayer to express your heart to God:

Father God, thank You for loving me and for sending Jesus, Your only begotten Son, to die in my place as a sacrifice for my sin.
Lord Jesus, I believe You died for me on the cross, that You shed your blood as a ransom for my soul, and that three days later you bodily rose again from the dead.
Please forgive me, come into my heart, and save me from myself and my sin. Deliver me from the powers of the world, the flesh, and the devil. In Jesus' name, amen.

COSTAS WOULD WANT YOU TO KNOW YOU CAN BE SURE

Friend, if you have trusted Christ for the forgiveness of your sins, the Bible says you can be assured of pardon and eternal life:

These things I have written unto you who believe in the name of the Son of God, so that you may *know* that you have eternal life. (1 John 5:13, emphasis mine)

We don't just *hope* we will be forgiven; God wants us to *know* we have forgiveness. God is who He says He is, and He keeps His promises. We can trust Him with this life and with eternity. He says to each of His children, "I will never desert you, nor will I ever forsake you" (Hebrews 13:5).

COSTAS WOULD WANT YOU TO BECOME A SURRENDERED DISCIPLE

All those that believe for salvation will encounter obstacles, as did Costas and Alky. Therefore, it is essential to follow the following guidelines:

- *Connect* to the Holy Spirit through prayer, as well as reading, meditation on, and memorization of the Word of God.

- *Connect* to a local church where the gospel is actively expressed through love and witness.

- *Commit* to the life of a surrendered disciple. Jesus said, "If anyone wishes to come after Me, he must deny himself, and take up his cross daily and follow Me" (Luke 9:23).

As you reflect on the story and principles you have read in *If I Had Two Lives,* will you choose to live a fully surrendered life with your time, talents, and treasure? I encourage you to express this to God, perhaps using the words of this prayer:

Lord Jesus, I surrender to You all that I am, all that I have, all that I ever hope to be. Use me as Your disciple to impact this world for the gospel and Your kingdom. In Jesus' name, amen.

In May 1986, when the trial of the 'Athens 3' was complete, Costas quickly exclaimed, **"Now I want five hundred missionaries for my country, to go to every town, every village, with this message of the gospel."** After more than thirty years the need is greater than ever. Could it be that God is calling you to join this great effort? Will you become a part of the five-hundred?

*   *   *

"For to me, to live is Christ and to die is gain."
—THE APOSTLE PAUL IN PHILIPPIANS 1:21

"Only one life, 'twill soon be past,
only what's done for Christ will last."
—C. T. STUDD

"He is no fool who gives what he
cannot keep to gain what he cannot lose."
—Jim Elliot

"If I had two lives to live . . . "
—Costas Macris

HELLENIC MINISTRIES
Christ for Greece and the Nations!

CIAL INITIATIVE - DISCIPLESHIP - OUTREACHES - MISSIONS

llenic Ministries exists that every person in Greece might have the opportunity to ow Jesus Christ personally, and thus impact their world as they serve Him with passion.

stas and Alky's vision was to see the nation of Greece re-evangelized with the gospel, d see young people run to the ends of the earth with this message of hope.

ward that end, Costas established a legacy fund for the purpose of leadership velopment, for scholarships for biblical training, and the support of national urch planters, evangelists and missionaries. Gifts to this fund can be designated way of the contact information below.

t our website **www.hellenicministries.org/give/** to see a variety of ways you can give
or **Greek bank account IBAN #: GR 73 0110 1040 0000 1044 8028 026**

▶W TO CONTACT US....

Greece: 12 Lydias St. 11527 Athens
@hellenicministries.org | Tel. +30 210 777 9845

HM US: PO Box 726, Wheaton, IL 60187-0726
hellenicministriesus@gmail.com | Tel. +1 630 520 0372

www.hellenicministries.org

ENDNOTES

1 For a complete history of Regions Beyond Missionary Union (RBMU), see the compelling account in Joseph F. Conley's *Drumbeats That Changed the World* (Pasadena: William Carey Library Publishers, 2000).

2 John Dekker and Lois Neely, *Torches of Joy* (Westchester, IL: Crossway, 1985), John's informative account of his and others' work with the Dani tribe.

3 Ephesians 5:20, KJV, emphasis and capitalization of "Name" added by Costas.

4 Don Richardson's exciting book *Peace Child* (Glendale, CA: G/L Regal, 1974) was instrumental in introducing many to missionary work among tribal cultures. His second book, *Lords of the Earth* (Glendale, CA: G/L Regal, 1977), continued in the same vein, recounting the advancement of the gospel through extreme sacrifice, even martyrdom. Both books contain important material on the life and ministry of the Macris family.

5 One can find a fascinating account of this expedition, including original videos, journals, and other source materials, by searching for the title "By Aeroplane to Pygmyland" at the Smithsonian Libraries online (www.sil.si.edu).

6 Matthew Stirling, By Aeroplane to Pgymyland, National Museum of Natural History, Smithsonian Institution, accessed 02/27/2017, http://www.sil.si.edu/expeditions/1926/JournalStirling/StirlingJournalOneDaySeq.cfm?id=74

7 visionary. Dictionary.com. *Dictionary.com Unabridged.* Random House, Inc. http://www.dictionary.com/browse/visionary, (accessed: February 27, 2017).

8 Margaret Truman, "Costas Macris, Man of Faith," *Reflections on an Unusual Journey* (blog), September 14, 2011, accessed March 1, 2017, http://reflectionsonanunusualjourney.blogspot.gr/2011/09/costas-macris-man-of-faith.html

9 Years later, Marina's father accepted Christ, largely due to the influence of Costas and the Macris family.

10 Don Stephens's book, *Trial by Trial* (Eugene, OR: Harvest House, 1985), describes the setting for the trial and details the *Anastasis*'s ministry around the world.

11 At the age of twenty two, Konstantine joined Mercy Ships, where he served for nine years, rising to the position of Director of International Programs. He then joined World Vision as a senior manager in both Eastern Congo and Bangladesh. His life has been dedicated to sharing God's love and compassion with those in need around the world. Konstantine currently lives in Northern Virginia, USA with his wife and four boys. The influence of Costas, Don and Alan upon his life remains a fundamental source of inspiration to this day.

12 The voyage is detailed in Kenneth R. Overman, *Dawn Passage: The Incredible Voyage of the Missionary Schooner, Morning Star* (West Conshohocken, PA: Infinity, 2010).

13 For Caleb's story, see Numbers 13–14 and Joshua 14:6–15 in the Old Testament.

DUE